When Jesus said, "The poor you will have with you always..." He surely didn't mean "...so don't care about them." In this moving account of serving in a downtown inner-city church where there are few easy answers, the author shares what surprising lesson she learned. A lesson that through "the least of these" we can—no, we must—learn. I heartily recommend this book.

—Rev. David S. Crawley

This book provides a look at a population living beside us that many have shunned or never acknowledged... every student of sociology and all support workers should read this book.

—Patricia Stott-Prince, M.Ed.

PEOPLE ARE NOT YOUR
PROBLEM
THEY ARE YOUR
Purpose

PEOPLE ARE NOT YOUR PROBLEM

THEY ARE YOUR

Purpose

Marcia Magee McClelland

PEOPLE ARE NOT YOUR PROBLEM,
THEY ARE YOUR PURPOSE
Copyright © 2022 by Marcia Magee McClelland

ISBN: 978-1-4866-2202-3
eBook ISBN: 978-1-4866-2203-0

Word Alive Press
119 De Baets Street Winnipeg, MB R2J 3R9
www.wordalivepress.ca

WORD ALIVE
—P R E S S—

Cataloguing in Publication information can be obtained from Library and Archives Canada.

This book is dedicated to all of those working in ministry to the homeless
and to the homeless people themselves who in their own way
teach us much about love and compassion.

Any profits from the sale of this book
will be used to support ministries that feed the homeless.

ACKNOWLEDGEMENTS

I WANT TO THANK REV. DAVID Crawley for reading the initial draft of this manuscript and offering his blessing on the project. I thank him as well for helping me grow in my spiritual journey during the years we worked together at Saint George's church.

I owe my husband Bill a big thank you for his encouragement and support for how he quietly and patiently allowed me the time and space to write and always showed an interest in how the project was progressing.

Thanks to my sister-in-law Patricia and my friend Freda for taking the time to read the original draft and offer their much-valued comments and suggestions.

A big thank you to the staff of Word Alive Press: Jen Jandavs-Hedlin, for her belief that this was a worthwhile project; to Ariana Forsman, the project manager who helped guide the publishing process; and a special thanks to Evan Braun, whose expertise and editing skills brought my words to life.

I have to thank the street friends whose stories are within these pages. To them I owe a huge debt of gratitude for changing my heart and opening my eyes to a better understanding and acceptance toward folks who live on our city streets.

Mostly, thank You, Father God, for laying this idea on my mind. May You be glorified through this writing.

INTRODUCTION

MANY YEARS AGO, I WAS WORKING for a privately owned stationery store in the downtown core of Ottawa, Ontario. As I took my daily walk to our bank to make deposits, I was often confronted by street people. When I first started the job, one fellow in particular was very pushy and often jumped out in front of me asking for "spare change." After this happened a few times, I became quite indignant. I even swore at him and told him angrily, "Leave me alone and don't bug me anymore!" From then on, he didn't request money, but he glared at me with a smirk, almost like he knew something I didn't.

In hindsight, I now believe he did. Many years later, I was to have an attitude change toward the vulnerable and fragile people who live on our city streets.

At the time of that incident, I wasn't a Christian and I had little sympathy for anyone I considered to be "in my way." What you will read in these pages is the story of how God changed my unsympathetic attitude and showed me that street people are *not* just bums who loved to hang out on the street and beg for money to buy drugs and alcohol.

Rather, these folks are God's children, just like me, only they've fallen on extremely hard times. Each and every person who's been forced to live on the streets has a very moving story, if we would only take the time to listen.

Ministering to street people was the farthest thing from my mind when I first worked in the city, but God knew what He had in mind… and He ultimately worked out His plan to teach me how much He loved them. Unbeknownst to me at that juncture, street folks would become a big part of my life.

God's plan sometimes takes a long, long time to unfold. He had a lot of work to do in me to prepare me for the time when I would become more involved with these vulnerable people. In fact, it wasn't until fifteen years later that God must have decided I was finally ready for the ministry He had in mind.

Two years after becoming a Christian, I left my well-paying secular job and was hired as the parish secretary for a large inner city church, which I'll affectionately refer to as Saint G's throughout this writing. I was to remain in that job for a period of thirteen years, eventually moving into the role of parish administrator.

During that time, there were many changes in the church itself, but the biggest change for me was my own attitude toward the people who lived on our city streets. Not only did I come to know them, but I can honestly say that some became my "street friends."

I record the words in this memoir as honestly and transparently as I can. Most of the information is gleaned from the personal journals I kept during those years. Many memories were sparked when I reread those journals.

This memoir isn't written in chronological order. Instead the stories are loosely organized according to how I feel they each relate to the themes which I've used as headings for each chapter. I use first names throughout, but note that in all cases I've changed the names of my street friends to protect their identities.

I also share the raw, often profound feelings we, the staff of our church, felt toward certain individuals—fear, frustration, anger, etc.—to show that we, too, although Christians, most definitely have normal human emotions that get stirred up when dealing with people.

Within these pages, I mention the beloved staff members I had the privilege of working with, those who were also involved in ministry to the fragile and vulnerable. First, our clergy: Rev. Dave and Rev.

Jennifer. Then the support staff: Bernie (maintenance) and Beth (office). And finally the casuals: Jack, Jim, and Bill, who all served as maintenance replacements when other staff were on vacation. Each of them in their own way was a blessing to our many drop-in folks.

Rev. Dave was the rector of Saint G's during my time working there. He was a tall man with reddish hair and a full beard, who had a gleam in his eye and knew how to laugh and make others laugh. He was also a man of solid Christian morals, with the innate ability to *really* listen to people. After talking to Rev. Dave, parishioners and others would often comment that they had known they had his undivided attention. He also had wise discernment about the real needs of others and knew how to guide his "flock" into using their God-given talents.

Rev. Jennifer joined the staff as associate priest two years after I started at the parish. She was a petite woman, newly arrived from England with her husband and two young sons. She worked closely with Rev. Dave and was gifted with strong preaching skills. Some parishioners nicknamed her the Sermonator! The women in the parish were delighted to have a female member of the clergy on board and she and Rev. Dave worked together to move the parish and the "sheep" forward.

Bernie was the perfect choice to be hired as sexton (maintenance/caretaker) for the building. Not only did he have exceptional cleaning skills, but he was naturally creative and was able to design and build any new projects that needed doing. Also, he daily made an urn of coffee for the staff and our drop-ins. The coffee was always on and made with love. He was a retired police officer, so his larger presence and expertise in dealing with troubled individuals proved helpful during some of the incidents that occurred at the church within this writing.

Beth joined the parish office as receptionist/secretary a few years into my time there. She was a blessing to our staff and congregation, and because of her missionary background she became an asset to our evangelizing programs as well.

It was a pleasure working with all these dedicated Christian workers.

Saint G's was a large Anglican church built in 1885. Its front had three entrances. The main one was a large wooden double door centred in front and open to the street. Then there were two concrete staircase entrances on either side, both of which had iron gates blocking them. I once asked Rev. Dave the reason for the gates and he explained that these two entries had become a place where street folks would camp out at night and sometimes light fires. Because these staircases had become a fire hazard, our insurance company had required that they be blocked off. The gates didn't look inviting to outsiders, but sadly they were necessary.

Upon entering through the main double doors at street level, a visitor would come to two sets of stairs, one on each side, which led up into the main sanctuary. One would then arrive at the sanctuary door to see a long, red-carpeted aisle stretching up to the main altar. An incredibly colourful stained-glass window arched its way up behind the altar to the peak of the roof. There were pews on both sides of the main aisle and several other impressive stained-glass windows on each side of the vast sanctuary.

Approaching the altar area, visitors would come to a raised step and a short ramp so that those with handicaps would be able to receive communion at the altar rail. An intricately carved pulpit was to the left. Then, looking back from the altar area, one could see the balcony at the back of the church. Exit stairs to the right of the altar led to the lower hall and the parish office, which was my home away from home for the next thirteen years.

THE BEGINNING
Jesus Is Coming, Look Busy!

MAY 1, 1999 IS THE DAY that my life of servanthood for the Lord really began. It was my first day working at Saint G's, and I prayed that I would be filled with the Holy Spirit to learn, listen, and *really* hear and see. I knew I had a lot to learn and wanted to keep an open heart and open mind. I asked God to remove my know-it-all attitude and help me with the church administration and with His people—the staff, congregation, and anyone else I should meet.

The words of the song "Here I Am, Lord" kept running through my mind and the tears of the Spirit flowed as I prayed early that first morning: "Thank You, Jesus. I need it to sink in that I don't have all the answers, that I can't solve everyone's problems and that I have to get my strength from You and give glory to You." I sensed this was going to be a very humbling experience.

"Today's the big day," my husband said as I left home. "Do me a favour and just be aware. This is a different crowd from the one you're used to dealing with."

I promised that I would, but I wondered why he would even speak those words.[1]

When I walked into the church office, the first thing I saw was a sign that said "Jesus Is Coming, Look Busy." It made me chuckle and put a big smile on my face! It also made me aware that of *all* the

---

[1] I was to understand his comment more fully as time went on.

bosses I've ever had in my life, at Saint G's I would be working for Jesus. He would know and see my every action.

In the office, I met Penny, the woman who would be training me. She was a church warden who had been filling in until I was hired. She instructed me to wear the "panic button," a necklace device with a red button that linked directly to our security company. When the button was pushed, the security company would contact the police, who would come and check the office and the rest of the building.

I dutifully put the necklace on, although I must admit I didn't like wearing it. I knew it was for my own protection, but it seemed to send an untrusting message to those entering the church. I wore it initially, but after a few months I just kept it close in my desk drawer.

I met my first street person within an hour of being in the parish office. Doug was a short man—in his late twenties, I estimated—with curly, reddish-blond hair, deep blue eyes, and a pleasant smile. He had his dog Sandy with him.

Doug had heard that Penny's work in the office would soon be over and wanted to give her a little aqua-coloured rock.

"I've had this a long time, but I want you to have it," he said.

Penny was very touched by the gesture, as was I.

That little rock probably means more to her than someone giving her a gold bracelet, I thought.

That's the moment when I realized, for the first time, that street folks have a heart and that we can befriend them and make them feel as special as they really are.

After a few days of Penny's expert training, I was on my own in the parish office and started learning not only about the administration of the church but about street ministry—through direct experience.

I also had to absorb Rev. Dave's advice: "Do not give them money, or you'll be giving them your whole paycheque, because they'll tug at your heartstrings from time to time. I have a discretionary fund that we can use for such purposes if need be.

For my first year in the parish office, this fund was dispersed only with Rev. Dave's approval. After that, he gave me permission to use it at my own discretion. He'd known that I had to go through a training period in wisdom and discernment first, otherwise I'd be handing out money for all the needs I saw!

A local woman who operated a street ministry arrived that morning to meet with Rev. Dave. While waiting for her meeting, we had a nice chat about life on the streets. She told me that she herself had been a street person, and afterward she had trained as a nurse. She'd been working on the streets for twenty years, using her street smarts and nursing skills to help others. She told me about "street codes" and "buying spots" (places to pan-handle), and taught me that some people on the streets have to pay "protection" to street gangs. The conversation I had with her was a real eye-opener for me!

She then gave me tips on protective ways to stand and how to position my arms as a defence.[2] She also suggested that I get a yearly test for tuberculosis (TB) and hepatitis (Hep B). She said that TB is airborne and is rampant on the street, and that *everyone* on the street has Hep B, which is passed through saliva. She also said that some have Hep A and Hep C, which is blood-related, and/or HIV. As I would be in contact with street people through my work, she explained that these tests were a precautionary measure.

She also shared a story about a rape and murder that happened once at a church. That was something I didn't need to hear! She then mentioned two planned suicides the previous week, of two guys who wanted to "go home to the Lord" together.

When our conversation ended, I had a lot of streetwise information to absorb. I prayed that I wouldn't feel fearful in my new position, but that I would always act with wisdom while ministering to the street folk who dropped in on a daily basis.

I also prayed that I could show Christ's love and compassion at all times. I gradually came to realize that this would be a challenge without God's help. Along with my official office duties, I was now in full-fledged training for street-folks ministry.

I also began to better understand the comment my husband had made early that morning.

---

[2] This helped me to understand why we had a half-door in the office, which could be securely locked from the inside.

GETTING TO KNOW THE STREET FOLK
They Are People Too

AFTER PENNY'S DEPARTURE FROM MY OFFICE training, Doug often came in with his dog—and some of my old cynicism started to arise. I worried about him being able to eat, and yet he could afford to feed his dog! Then he also talked about feeding a muffin to the birds. I had been planning to buy him a coffee that morning, and I questioned myself since he seemed able to feed the birds with a muffin he bought…

Through this, I came to realize that I had tended to measure my charity in the past. I hadn't given from a loving heart.

When I came out of the local coffee shop the next morning, Doug was outside and showed me a box of squares that a woman had given him along with five dollars for his birthday. I felt like a heel. I had a *lot* to learn about actual ministry and the compassion that needs to go with it!

Doug continued to visit, as he had been staying in a near-by shelter. One day he told me that he was moving back onto the street for the summer. My husband had once mused that he thought people like him actually preferred to live on the street, and this made me think he might be right.

Sometime later, while there was an election going on, we had a polling station at the church and Doug came in to cast a vote. But the poll workers wouldn't allow him to, as he had no legal address.

He became angry and got very down on life. I tried to encourage him, but he said, "If I had a gun, I'd kill myself!"

"Don't talk like that," I urged him.

"It's just the way I feel!"

As he was walking out, I spontaneously said, "We love you!"

I hoped he'd heard that.

A few days later, just as I left the church for the day, Doug showed up wanting to go back inside to make a call. There was another man with him, so I told him that the call would have to wait. I wasn't prepared to go back into the church alone with two men.

He became upset.

Another day, he entered the lobby and was quite mouthy, swearing on the phone loud enough so I could hear. I locked the office and went into the church thinking, *I'm not going to give him an audience. I don't need to listen to that!*

I then didn't see Doug in a while, but he showed up one day to say that Christmas Eve would be his last day on the streets, as he had a new apartment. He had gotten his life together and would apparently never be on the streets again.

I hoped so, for his sake.

But it wasn't long before we saw him again, and sadly he was very angry. He said he was ready to buy a gun to kill others and himself. I tried to talk to him, as did one of our wardens, but he was so upset. He commented that he was really trying but felt the world was against him.

Rev. Dave overheard our conversation, then talked to him and eventually calmed him down. He also agreed to go take a look at Doug's new place to discern his needs and see how the church could help. Rev. Dave always went where he was needed, even if he was physically exhausted from other church work. His genuine concern helped put Doug in a better mood.

A few days later, Doug returned and gave me a little heart pin. He thanked me and called me a friend, and Rev. Dave as well. That was heart-warming to hear. I told him that I'd treasure the little heart and wear it on my lapel.

"I know you will," he replied.

The next time we saw him, he had shaved his head bald. He told me had to leave his apartment at the end of that week and really just needed to talk to someone.

"Prayer didn't work," he said sadly.

"Do you pray?" I asked.

"No."

"Then it can't work. May I pray with you?"

He agreed.

I don't know what I actually said, but I trusted the Holy Spirit to lead and Doug seemed calmer afterward. He told me that he was going home to pack and would be returning to the streets for a month or so until he found another place.

I was concerned for him, because he needed a physical address to keep his disability pension.

Again, it was a while before Doug dropped in. I had continued to pray for him, though, since I was concerned that he may have done harm to himself; he had once told me that he self-inflicted when angry.

As I took the mail across the street one day, there he was with his dog coming toward me. Thank You, Jesus! We chatted and he explained that he'd gotten another small apartment and had been busy. He was in good spirits and seemed positive and upbeat. I was happy for him.

We shook hands and wished each other Happy Easter. It was good to know that he was okay. It was an answer to prayer.

But sadly, a few months later he once again got thrown out of his apartment. He told me he was hitting the road and was going to hitchhike with his dog, but didn't know where he would go. I doubted he would leave, thinking sadly that this was just the plan of the week and that it would probably change. He was leading such a sad life.

Around this time, I had a sleeping bag stashed in my car for a couple of months. One morning I happened to take it out and put it on the chair in the church hall, to donate to someone. This also happened to be the day of Doug's next visit.

When Doug saw it, he said, "I've been looking for a sleeping bag!"

But he also said that the world just hadn't been going right for him lately. He didn't seem to recognize that God *had* taken care of him that day, by providing the sleeping bag. It was a small example of God's care, but it was His care nonetheless.

He rambled a lot that morning. I prayed and sensed God speak to my heart, *"He just needs someone to listen today."* So in obedience, I stopped what I was doing and just listened.

Another day, Doug came in clean-shaven and well-dressed, wearing a newer jacket with a poppy on his lapel. He told me he had been in court. I gave him a couple of pairs of new long johns from our clothing donation room, as the weather had been turning colder.

At the time he came in, I happened to be installing new shelves in the church office, so I asked if he could help me. He seemed pleased to be asked and said, "Any time."[3] Things seemed to be looking up for him and I gave him a hug. It was nice to see him smile.

In the new year, I looked out the church office window one day to see Doug being chased away from the laneway by police. The officer then came in to let me know that he couldn't panhandle outside anymore or he'd be sent to jail.

This officer needs compassion, I thought. *It's a tough life on the streets.*

My heart went out to Doug.

The next time he showed up, we had a long and chatty visit. He had a deep, chesty cough and I worried he may have developed pneumonia, or TB. I gave him all the change in my car's coin-holder so he could eat and get some hot coffee over the upcoming weekend. He separated out the pennies and told me that he always gave them to the Children's Wish Foundation.

He had a good heart, and it's sad that he had to lead such a rough day-to-day life. It made me realize just how blessed I was. On that cold, damp day, I could go home to my cozy house and curl up by the fire. I admonished myself for ever complaining.

Eventually Doug popped in to say goodbye and to tell us he was leaving for Calgary. I'm not sure if he ever did go, but we never saw him again.

---

[3] Street friends need to be needed.

He was my first introduction to street friends. I was to meet many, many more over the years. Some of them were delightful to meet while others could be frustrating and at times even worrisome.

I met many different personalities, and although all were needy in their own particular way, some were just one-timers, dropping by for a particular need and never to be seen again. Others were addicts, or delusional, or angry, or even downright evil.

Then there were those seeking to know more about the God we served.

After a time, I realized that my own personality would change depending on the person and the day. I could be either happy, dopey, sleepy, grumpy, etc… I liked it when I was in the *happy* role and felt bad when I was in the *grumpy* role. Sadly, it did happen from time to time with certain folks. I found that by sitting in total silence in the early morning, alone in the church chancel, I could best prepare for the day. This helped me in my interactions with people, even in the midst of busyness. I also found value in putting on the whole armour of God and reading Ephesians 6:10–20 on a daily basis.

Along with my regular administrative duties, I knew I was there to serve the weak and the vulnerable… and I would have to constantly rely on His strength and wisdom. I sensed that at Saint G's, we weren't here to reinvent the wheel for the homeless; we were to enhance the work already being done by other street ministry groups in the city, to continue our outreach and hopefully in so doing introduce them to Jesus.

Our church mission statement was "Transforming broken lives into world-changing disciples." Whatever God wanted, He would achieve. It seemed He wanted only my willingness. I placed this new role in His most capable hands and prayed, "Lord, equip me."

THE FRIENDLY AND FUNNY ONES
Smiles in Our Day

GOD ALWAYS MADE PROVISION FOR THE lost souls on our streets. He had created them, He wanted them back, and our role was to minister to them. We were in this inner-city area for a reason.

I didn't know what God's plan was for Saint G's, but I knew we could never neglect the ministry to our street friends. If God wanted me involved, I needed to be obedient and humble myself to do the work He'd called me to do. God knew I needed humbling, and He also knew that I'd always wanted to help those less fortunate.

Help me, Lord, to see Your vision for this place, I prayed. *I want something that will light my fire, not burn me out as I help others.*

Street folks have it tough just getting food, lodging, and clothing. They helped me to understand that we need to be content with what God has given us. We have so much more than people on the street have. I prayed that the Lord would help those we served throughout the week to come to know Jesus as their true Saviour, and I prayed for us to be thankful for His provision in our own lives, so we could help others with the blessings we'd received.

Some of the street friends we met over the years brought smiles to our faces with their daily visits and helped lighten up the atmosphere of this often difficult ministry. In spite of their desperate circumstances, some had a great sense of humour and were able to give us a better understanding of joyfulness in spite of lack.

In this chapter, I'll share a few of the funny stories.

A very drunk fellow once sat on our laneway steps just outside the office window, loudly singing "O Suzanna," and quite off-tune! I didn't mind that, but when he started swigging a bottle of beer, I asked God what I should do.

The singing is fine, I sensed the Lord say to me. *But the beer on the church stairs has to go!*

So I went outside and asked him to move on. He broke into singing "Praise the Lord" and started calling me "sister." I knew I couldn't reason with him in his drunken state, so I just smiled and said, "Move on, God bless." With that, I closed the church door.

He hung around on the steps for a little while longer, then hid the beer in his coat and weaved his way across the busy street in heavy traffic! Another drunken fellow joined him.

This was my first real introduction to street alcoholics and it led to my first altercation later that same day. As I was leaving work, another street person showed up and asked, "Did you call the police?" Apparently he'd heard that I had threatened to call the police on the drunken fellow I'd met earlier that day. Anyway, I assured him that I hadn't; I'd just moved him on because of the beer.

This altercation helped me to realize that street people look out for each other.

Moe was one of my favourite regulars. He was a middle-aged man, tall and thin, with long, black curly hair and a pointy nose. His dark brown eyes glistened when he smiled, and what a smile he had!

The first time Moe came in, he said that he needed cash. We talked and I felt compelled to give him ten dollars. I didn't usually do that, but for some reason that day I did. Then he prayed for me, to Allah, and I thanked him and prayed in return to Jesus.

"You look taller when you're sitting there," he said, smiling as he pointed to my desk chair.

This comment cracked me up. It was such a funny observation of my short stature compared to his tall lankiness!

Moe came in almost daily to chat about all his ills, and one day he told me that I was helping him spiritually. I liked to believe this was true. All I knew was that over the length of his visits, what he really *always* wanted was bus tickets. He'd chitchat, then asked for two bus tickets. Always two. I found that rather funny; no matter what the topic of the day, it would always come down to the bus tickets.

Another fellow who proved to be quite an amazing surprise came to the office for a period of about two weeks, always coming around the same time early in the morning. He was slight in build and wore a pleasant smile despite his dishevelled appearance. He didn't want to give his name, and, respecting his privacy, I didn't press for him to tell me.[4]

He asked if he could play the piano in the church and I told him that we didn't allow that, but there was one in the upper hall he was welcome to use for half an hour. He was pleased and I unlocked the door to the upper hall to give him access.

Within a few minutes, I was astounded to hear the most beautiful sounds coming out of that old piano! I knew there were no music sheets or books, so he had to be playing by ear.

The classical music flowed so fluidly that it brought tears to my eyes. I rushed to gather the other staff and volunteers in the building so they could share in this incredible gift. We sat in the foyer listening until the music stopped. Then, so not to embarrass this fellow, we all went back to our work areas and tasks before he re-entered the lobby.

I let the young man know just how much we had enjoyed his music. He seemed pleased, yet remained shy and cautious. He asked if he could return another day to play, and we were blessed with his talents several times during those two weeks.

After that, we never saw him again, nor did he ever reveal his name. I pray he is well and using his incredible God-given gift.

Jakov was another likeable fellow. He was a tall, broad-shouldered man with a thick Croatian accent. I had to listen really closely to understand what it was he wanted.

Initially he came in for some food, and he also asked for five dollars. We made him a sandwich and gave him a hot coffee. This went on for several days until we directed him to the other ministries that provided meals.

---

[4] Some street folks took more time than others to build trust.

He often showed up in church on Sundays for the after-service hospitality treats and usually asked parishioners for five dollars. He was always pleasant and polite.

After chatting with him several times, I discovered that he was artistic and liked to paint. As I had a surplus of art supplies at home, I brought in some paper, paints, and brushes to give him as an encouragement in his creativity. He sometimes brought some of his work to show me and Beth, and we hung a couple of his works in the office.

He started to attend the full church service, not just showing up for the hospitality time. He would take a place in the pew and seemingly enjoyed the service, gaining a sense of belonging from being among other parishioners.

THE PRACTICAL AND NEEDY
Soup, Sandwiches, Love, and Boundaries

I FELT BLESSED YET CHALLENGED AT times by the opportunity to minister to those in need. It was a big and very rewarding part of my work, especially when I knew I'd been able, by God's grace and through the generosity of the Saint G's community, to assist someone desperately in need and then see their face light up with relief. I learned that kindness, with compassion, is indeed a fruit of the Spirit. Our street friends needed to know that Saint G's was a loving, welcoming place.

The challenging part is that I felt frustrated some days with the needs of our regular street folk. I didn't really want to listen to their same constant needs again and again. Then I'd remember that Jesus had compassion for everyone and I'd listen once more. On those particular days, myself and the other staff needed to sense His heart and be filled with His grace.

We also learned that at times we needed to set certain boundaries and direct folks to agencies that were more capable of fulfilling their practical needs.

Marcella was a dark-haired woman whom I estimated to be in her late thirties. She also had a thick French accent. She rang the back doorbell one day and needed money (ten dollars) for a baby she said was diabetic. I felt bad, but had to let her know that Rev. Dave was out and I wasn't authorized to give out money.

This was the hardest part of the job, because you never knew if you were turning away a real need or a fake one.

I told her that I'd pray for her and her baby. She thanked me.

Marcella came back several times for various needs: food for the baby, feminine products for herself, and prescriptions. Rev. Dave often met these needs from his rector's discretionary fund and one of us staff would walk to the store or pharmacy and pay the costs.

Eventually Marcella stopped coming to the parish office.

A black gentleman came in to see "the priest" one day. He needed money to eat and asked for one or two dollars. I felt my heart being tugged when I said, "I'm sorry, I'm not authorized to give out money." I recommended the local soup kitchen, the food bank, and a couple of other nearby ministries for men in the city. I also invited him to our Friday evening drop-in for soup and sandwiches. He said he couldn't come back then, as he'd be too tired walking on his one good leg.

I tried to encourage him, yet it seemed so futile.

"I'll pray for you," I said as he walked away.

He thanked me and I almost cried. I couldn't get him off my mind. I kept recalling Mother Teresa's words: "See Jesus in everyone you meet." I felt like I had just shut the door in Jesus's face. The church was meant to help, and with this man we hadn't.

In spite of not having had access to the rector's discretionary fund at that time, I could have personally met his immediate need of food/money from my own resources. Yes, I prayed, but I felt that I had let him down—and therefore let Jesus down. The ministry to street folk was difficult at times!

I talked to Rev. Dave about my feelings on this and he said, "You were put here to meet other needs for them. Remember, Jesus didn't give to everyone who asked or begged. We can only do what we can do. We must leave the rest in God's hands."

Rev. Dave used the example of the blind beggar (Mark 10:46–52) and the woman who touched Jesus's robe (Luke 8:43–48). These examples from Scripture made sense to me and his words spoke to my spirit, making me feel much better. I came to understand that Jesus wants to heal the *whole* person.

I was grateful for Rev. Dave's wisdom and experience as I learned more about street-friend ministry.

Another needy person was Stanley, a very dishevelled-looking fellow with long curly brown hair and vivid blue eyes. When he came in, he was wearing a long woollen coat that was badly worn with rips and holes in it. Yet there seemed to be an intellectual man beneath that coat. He was always soft-spoken and he had a gentle demeanour. He came in hungry, so I went to the lower hall kitchen and made him a peanut butter sandwich.

One morning as I arrived early to open the church, I saw a fellow wrapped in blankets, lying on cardboard, tucked in the corner of the laneway. His head was covered, so I didn't know who he was.

As I entered the church, he awoke. So not to embarrass him, and feeling a little fearful being alone, I went quickly into the building.

Looking out the window, though, I realized that the man was Stanley and I wished I'd remained outside and brought him a coffee and muffin. It had been *so* cold that previous night, and he'd dragged his blankets and cardboard there to try to keep warm. I hoped Stanley would be okay and thanked God for my warm bed and beautiful home.

I prayed for Stanley and his loneliness, knowing that he was someone's relative—perhaps a son, brother, sister, or husband. This made me feel very sad. I asked God to help us at Saint G's not to forget the forgotten on our city streets. We had to honour our ministry to these fragile people. And I sensed God lay on my heart, *"I love them too."*

Our ministry for them always had to be a big part of what we were about as a church—and not just at our Friday night drop-in program, but more in-depth.

Stanley continued to drop in from time to time, saying hello and getting his peanut butter sandwich. One day he added a bright spot to my day when he brought me two bright yellow petunias. I thanked him and chuckled to myself; the roots were still attached so he'd obviously pulled them out of a garden somewhere along the route to the church!

I didn't see Stanley for a while, and then one day I received a call from him. He was in the hospital in another city. He sounded lucid and wanted me to call a padre he knew to ask him to be his power of attorney and get him transferred to a local hospital back in Ottawa. I promised I'd try.

I managed to contact the place where the padre was staying, but the nurse there told me, "Padre is ninety-two, has Alzheimer's, and can't remember what he had for lunch!"

I then spoke with Rev. Jennifer and it was decided that I shouldn't call Stanley back, but rather wait to see if he called again. Then I'd relay to him the padre's condition.

It was sadly obvious to me that Stanley himself wasn't as lucid as I'd first thought when he initially called. It would be a long time until I heard back from Stanley, which I'll mention later in the book.

THE ADDICTED
A Desire to Be Clean, But...

MANY OF OUR DROP-INS WERE addicted to drugs and alcohol. These were the folks who tugged at our hearts. They so wanted to be clean. They missed their families and we became like family to them. Yet as laypeople all we could really do was offer them love and try to meet their practical needs.

It wasn't unusual for them to come in either on a high or very depressed. They would use the lobby phone (for local calls only) to get in touch with family members and ask if they could receive financial help. Some would cry, desperate to return home, and through their tears they would mumble to the family member on the other end that they were really trying to stay clean and sober. Often these addicted folks would ask us to provide bus tickets to help them get home.

Our policy was *always* to get a family contact name and number, and then we would call and ask their permission first before responding to the request. In many instances, the person wasn't wanted back home because their addictive behaviour was a disruption to the whole family. Sadly, we would have to turn the individual down; this was always so hard to do.

Then again, it must have been even more difficult for family to have to deny their request.

As a mother, my heart ached for those who pleaded with their moms to give them another chance. I wondered what I would have done under the same circumstances. I recalled talking to a couple of mothers of street folk, and it was obvious that they loved their adult children, but they had tried so many times to reconcile the situation and had become physically and mentally exhausted.

Tina was a panhandler, a tall, dark-haired young woman. She was large-boned and had glazed eyes, one of which was predominately off to one side of her face. Also, she was *very* pregnant.

She was extremely loud the first time she came into the church office lobby, and usually gregarious every time thereafter. She had previously been given permission to use the bathroom and the hall phone. I always had to ask her to keep her voice down and request that she step back from the office door so I could better hear incoming phone calls. Rev. Dave warned me that this wasn't the first time she had shown up pregnant. It was also obvious that she was using drugs or alcohol.

One day she came in to let me know that it would be her birthday the following day. I thought it would be a nice gesture to give her a small token. The next day she came in wearing a rare smile. I wished her a happy birthday.

"Did you get me a surprise?" she asked.

"I did, but I apologize, I forgot it at home. However, I do have this little booklet for you."

Then I handed her a booklet entitled "Why Jesus?"

She took it then asked, "What time should I come tomorrow to get my gift?"

"The same time," I replied. "But it's not much, you know. Just a little something."

"That's okay," she said, and then left.

I wondered why I had forgotten her little gift and sensed, *"All she wants is love, someone to care."*

I had been told that she wasn't very sociable but I discovered that she really liked to talk. She told me that her boyfriend was in the Toronto area at his sister's with their two little girls and that she missed them all very much. She also said that the girls were ages two and one and that the new baby would be born in a couple of months.

The truth is, I'd already heard from our clergy that the Children's Aid Society had taken the previous children from her and they were actually ages six and seven. Perhaps, in her own mind, she was dreaming of where she would like the children to be. It was obvious that she wouldn't have been an attentive mother to them. But as long as she kept coming in, I made it a point to treat her with respect, smile, and chat. I believed that God had a purpose in every encounter.

Tina didn't show up the next day to collect her gift, but rather appeared the following day. I knew she was expecting money, but I gave her a birthday card and a little angel pin. She thanked me, then got on the phone and asked someone for fifty dollars to help her get food. I felt badly that I hadn't met her desperate need, and on my drive home I cried and prayed for Tina and others like her in such dire situations. I needed God's comfort to understand how to discern real needs from His perspective.

In the sanctuary early the next morning, I prayed for Tina and asked God to fill me with His grace. I thanked Him for the work He'd given me at the church and for His patience with me as I learned more about this ministry to street friends. I felt an inner calmness as tears filled my eyes and poured down my cheeks. I felt peaceful again and had a new step to my day.

During the period of time Tina was dropping in at the church, she delivered her third baby and went on to have yet another pregnancy. Then suddenly she just stopped showing up. I had to assume she must have moved out of the city.

Marc was a young man in his late twenties, and he also had addiction issues, but underneath the addiction was a gentle soul. He often visited, looking for warm clothes and to use the hall phone to call his mother who lived outside the city. They would chat and I'd hear him say, "I love you too, Mom." As a mom myself, I often thought about how her heart must have ached for her son and his safekeeping.

One day he showed up in extremely rough shape. He didn't have a shirt on and said he was in pain. He still had tabs on his chest from a recent electrocardiogram and he wanted to go back to the clinic where he'd gotten the test. Jim, who was covering our maintenance duties that day, drove him there.

The pain must be from his liver, as he's usually drunk all the time, I thought to myself. *So sad.*

After many months of visiting us off and on for his various needs, he came in embarrassed because he was so dirty. My husband happened to be covering the maintenance duties that day.

"Bill is my husband," I told Marc. "You can trust him."

So he followed Bill to the clothing room. After getting cleaned up, as Marc was leaving, he said to me, "I love you."[5]

One morning Marc was heavily on my mind, as I hadn't seen him in a while. So I prayed for him.

Then I received word from another local ministry worker that Marc had suffered a seizure and had fallen down a steep set of stairs and died. My heart was filled with sorrow for this precious child of God and I wept!

---

[5] The short time Bill worked at the church was an eye-opening experience for him. He learned that street folk are people too, not just "bums" as he had previously labelled them. Bill came to know they had heart, soul, feeling, and had just fallen on hard times.

THE DELUSIONAL AND SCHIZOPHRENIC
Things Are Not as They Seem

MY DAILY BIBLE LESSON ONE MORNING came from Galatians 6:2: *"Bear one another's burdens, and so fulfill the law of Christ."* I had come to learn that some of the street people were schizophrenic and acted much differently when off their medications. These folks were among the most difficult types to deal with as their personalities would fluctuate, often during the same day. They strained our ability to cope, since we weren't trained for their type of illness. But we managed to try befriending them by God's grace.

One particular day was like a zoo, loud and noisy. I was *not* coping well. I tried to be polite but wished everyone would just go away so I could get my administrative work done. I needed quiet!

I asked God to help me be humble. I needed God's grace.

I had planned to spend the day catching up, but instead I had ten pastoral care issues to handle and the atmosphere in the parish office became crazy.

In my frustration of trying to get caught up on my regular duties, I prayerfully lamented the disruptions of the day. Then I gently sensed God impress on my heart, *"People are not your problem. They are your purpose."*

I was very quickly humbled.

It seemed that on this one day *all* the delusional ones were in need! But after hours, I had to turn them away as I was alone in the building. I ended my workday with some of them singing and drinking on the laneway stairs.

In spite of it all, as I got in my car and headed home I was able to say to myself, *Thank You, Father, for the privilege of working in this place. I know You have called me here for Your purposes—and that is enough.*

Many more times throughout the years, I had to remember that God was with me and He would strengthen me for the tasks He had given me, that it was *His* strength through His Holy Spirit that was operating, not mine. I know I said "But Lord" a lot, yet He reminded me in Scripture, *"I will be with you."*

Don was another one of our regulars. He was civil and friendly.

The first time I met him, he needed clothes. He was happy to take a sweater and asked Rev. Dave if we had any toques. We did have some, and Rev. Dave placed one on Don's head. Then Don "blessed" us.

After he departed, Rev. Dave said, "That's the most civil conversation I've had with Don since I've known him!" He also told me that Don was a university graduate and that his father was a prominent person in our city.[6]

Don dropped into the church office from time to time. For the most part he was rational, but on other occasions he definitely wasn't. One day, the Altar Guild lady came in and asked me to talk to him, because he had placed a salad on the altar. I told him that he knew he wasn't to do that because the altar is a sacred place. With an impish twinkle in his eye, he admitted to doing it and said something about "sacrificing for the demons."

I often saw Don in his spot as I walked to and from parish errands. One day he came in with socks and mittens on his feet and I knew that someone at the men's shelter must have stolen his boots, yet again. I gave him a pair of unused donated shoes. He then hugged them and said, "Are they shoes, darlin?" He then hugged them again.

---

[6] I found that so sad. Don's situation reminded me of a fellow back home in New Brunswick who used to write algebra and physics formulas on the side of the bus shelter, yet he lived in the mental institution on the hill near that same bus shelter.

As of this writing, it's been a few years since I've worked at the church. Yet while attending a recent funeral, I saw Don still on the street, only sitting in a new spot.

Another man, Dale, came in one day and had obviously been drinking, though he vehemently denied it. He told me that he was forty-four, in pain, and had brain damage. He wanted to get a bus ticket to Halifax to go home to his mother.

I prayed silently for the Holy Spirit's help and discernment, then calmly took his ID, got his mother's phone number in Nova Scotia, and called her while he waited outside.

His story did check out, but his mother wasn't ready for him to come home, as his drinking always became violent and disrupted the family. She was preparing to go on a two-week vacation and got upset, not knowing know what to do. I reassured her that I didn't want to cause her undue stress and agreed to tell him that no one would be home right then. His mother and I agreed that if in two weeks he still wanted to go home, he could come back to the church and make a new request. Dale thought that was a good idea because he'd have his government rebate cheque by then as well—and his mother felt he'd sober up and change his mind.

Two weeks later, he did come back. I'd prayed for God's guidance in case he did.

He said that he'd spoken to his mom, so I called her again. She was now more open to him returning and said quietly, "He's my son."

That's all I needed to hear.

We agreed he would be on his way back to Halifax. I knew God had guided the whole process. It was times like these that were most gratifying. I knew I was somehow involved in doing God's work by serving His beloved street people.

A couple of days later, I received a call from the pastor of a local men's ministry who knew Dale. He wanted to thank our church for sending him home to Halifax. He said they'd been working with him for a while and believed he sincerely wanted to quit drinking and have a fresh start.

"It's so nice to see God using both of us at the same time to help someone," the pastor said. "God truly had a hand in this."

I, too, believed He did!

It was also interesting that this pastor had given Dale a small Bible for his journey home, and I had given him a daily inspirational booklet. God uses many people at the same time to help meet another's needs.

Several months later, I was very surprised to see Dale walk into the church. He asked if I remembered him and I replied, "Of course! How was Nova Scotia?"

"Okay," he said. "Not great."

He'd stayed two months, but it didn't work out with his mother. So he'd hitchhiked back, which took him four days. He now wondered if he'd ever see his mother again.

"I just wanted to come and say thank you for sending me home," he said in his drunken state.

I told him he was very welcome. Then I felt led to give him the current daily inspirational booklet. "This is to help you each day you're back on the street and to let you know that God loves you, Dale."

He left with a smile, back onto the streets.

Clem was another needy street person. He was an Indigenous fellow with long dark hair and full beard. He was on the laneway stairs when I arrived for work. He had a large bottle of mouthwash with him, a powerful alcohol substitute for some people.

"I just woke up," he said, sounding afraid. "I go now."

My unexpected presence seemed to have frightened him somewhat and he left quickly.

When I arrived the next day, he was sound asleep under the stairs roof, protected from the rain.

Lord, he feels safe and dry there and I've just come from a warm, comfy bed...

I said good morning a couple of times, then raised my voice a bit louder so he would hear me. He awoke startled and prepared to move.

I tried to ease his initial panic. "Were you dry and comfortable?"

He said that he was and I asked if he was going to the Mission for breakfast. I prayed he would go there and take advantage of their hot meals.

Clem was on the stairs again the next day. I woke him and gave him two dollars for a hot coffee—although, cynically, I suspected he'd use it to buy alcohol-based mouthwash.

Eddie was a well-dressed man who wanted to see the priest. Initially he talked about his teeth, or lack of them. He was an attractive man for his age—he told me he was sixty-five—but he was troubled and wanted to talk.

However, as we got into the conversation, with me listening and him talking, it became very obvious that he believed he was Jesus! It was a little scary, as this was my first experience with someone who was that delusional.

"You may even be an angel," he said, "but read Isaiah 53 and you'll know."

He talked about the "ten" in Scripture being a reference to the provinces of Canada and added that if he divulged all he knew, then many politicians would go to jail… including his own sister. He rambled from one topic to the next.

I knew he'd spend the day talking if he could, so I had to find a way to close the conversation. I prayed silently for the Holy Spirit's help and gently reminded him that the priest was unable to see him that day, but that he could call first thing in the morning.

"I have work to finish," I said apologetically. "I'll pray that you get the help you need for your teeth."

And I silently prayed that he'd get the mental help he needed as well.

Eddie did drop in again. It was sad to see someone so delusional and paranoid. Yet he looked so "normal." He got agitated because Rev. Dave wasn't available, so he left…and then came back again. This time, Rev. Dave said he could only give him five minutes; he gave him fifteen. Afterward, Rev. Dave and I prayed together.

We didn't see him again and I often wondered what became of him.

Kaydee phoned he church several times to talk to the priest. Then she eventually came in. On the phone, she seemed to have an older voice, and I was surprised to discover that she was probably only in her mid-forties. She was slender with brown hair and looked fairly attractive.

On the phone, she had expressed practical needs, yet talking to her in person she seemed to have a grasp of Scripture and appeared more spiritual. She told me that she had just moved downtown.

We initially had a nice chat over a cup of tea, but I was soon to learn just how needy and *unspiritual* she really was.

She said that she was upset and wanted to pray with Rev. Dave, but he wasn't around so I suggested that I could pray with her instead. We prayed, then she left.

When Rev. Dave arrived later in the day, I told him about my encounter with her.

"You'd probably be better for her than me," he said, adding that he had to learn to be careful with the demands he got from all the Kaydees of the world. He also mentioned that she was a referral and had *lots* of issues.

"I don't want her burdening you with all her problems either," he said. "A cup of tea is nice, now and then, but she can't make a habit of that."

One day Kaydee called, sounding excited that she'd found an apartment. Although she still had no job at that point. It was nice to hear a change in the tone of her voice and I told her so. She also wanted to ask me a question[7] about God and the nature of the Trinity: the Father, the Son, and the Holy Spirit.

"Some people say they are 'separate' persons," she said.

"Separate is a poor choice of word," I told her. "It's rather like a vast ocean with rivers, lakes, and streams running off it, but all are really part of that same ocean."

She liked that and I thanked God for His guidance in providing me with those words.

Kaydee started calling almost daily for issues such as finding work, fibromyalgia pain, spiritual questions, and requests to pray over the phone. Her constant calls were becoming a problem and taking up a lot of time. Rev. Dave was also getting frustrated with her and began to see a pattern forming.

---

[7] I prayed for the right words and found them with the Holy Spirit's help!

One day she called to leave a message for Rev. Dave, and in it she told him about a vision she claimed that Jesus had given her the previous night. The vision left her "concerned."

Rev. Dave shook his head. "I don't doubt the vision, but I'd like to see more *fruit.*"

That made sense, because we could see that Kaydee was into what God was doing in her life, but she wasn't using her gifts to serve others.

Another day, she called three times within ten minutes and then arrived for more prayer and anointing. I wondered if her needs could ever be met and what role God wanted us to continue to play in her journey.[8]

After many prayer times and anointing with healing oil, Rev. Dave discerned that he believed Kaydee was *addicted* to prayer ministry. He and a member of our prayer team were going to pray with Kaydee for release from all of this. He said he'd reached the point where he really didn't know what to do with her and we needed to wean her from ongoing prayer, as she was *too* needy at times.

Once we started the weaning process, she got very upset with Rev. Dave and eventually called to announce that she was heading off to Calgary. We thought it was all in her head, but a few weeks later Rev. Dave got a call from a priest in Calgary asking about Kaydee.

Interestingly, we weren't surprised by the nature of the call. It turned out she was living through the same pattern out west!

A few months later, one of our parishioners phoned to say she'd received a call from Kaydee asking for financial help. Apparently she'd lost her job and was planning to return to Ottawa.

Rev. Dave and I were both upset to hear this. Sadly, just hearing her name sucked the energy out of both of us.

Rev. Dave suggested to our parishioner that she *not* give any money, as this was an ongoing pattern with her. Kaydee had received a lot of genuine love at Saint G's, but she had left us all emotionally and physically drained.

---

[8] On a personal level, I thought perhaps God was trying to build more patience and compassion within me, as I tended to lack these characteristics after going through the same old, same old with Kaydee.

"We need to set limits so we don't get caught up in that again," Rev. Dave said.

Kaydee arrived back in the city and called a couple of times for prayer needs. Then, because she had settled into a different community, we no longer heard from her.

Another delusional person we met was Sandy. She came in one day rambling on about Kathryn Khulman, a late Christian minister known for her amazing healing services, and also about a present-day television evangelist. Sandy ranted on with sexual overtures about the evangelist and blasphemed the Holy Spirit.

As she talked, I silently prayed that the Holy Spirit would give me the words I needed to help calm her. I found myself speaking quietly, gently quoting Bible passages that helped her to settle down. The Holy Spirit also led me to pray with her and helped end the conversation with gentle reassurance for her.

I prepared myself for potential future visits, but she never returned.

Cindy was one of the *most* delusional people I met while working in the parish. She came into the church a very troubled woman with an incredible, hard-to-believe story. According to her, she was hiding from people who sought to do her harm. She told me that she was heading to a hermitage for her own safety and asked for prayer. I prayed with her for the protection she sought—and after she left, I quietly prayed for her mental state as well.

I didn't think much about Cindy after her first visit, but then she came back to say that the hermitage hadn't worked out. My heart ached for her, yet my mind swirled in disbelief that she felt so threatened.

Father, I need to know what this is all about with Cindy, I prayed silently. *Is this all true? If so, how do we proceed to help her? I need wisdom. Help me to not try to solve anything on my own. Please guide me and give us, the church, the steps to take, if any at all. I know You have a perfect plan in mind for Cindy. I know You will lead us in the right way to act on her behalf.*

I knew I had to have trust in His leading and at the same time be gracious and patient with her.

Rev. Dave told Cindy that he'd be willing to meet with her if I could be part of the meeting as well. He didn't want to be alone with her in case there were deep mental issues. Cindy also gave him some references to call, including an Orthodox priest and a bishop, but neither one returned Rev. Dave's calls prior to our meeting with her.

So we listened intently to her story about hiding from others and the harm she felt they wanted to do to her. Then we prayed with her. I prayed that she would find the freedom she deserved.

After meeting with her a couple of times, Cindy gave Rev. Dave another contact to assist in verifying her story. It was an email address for a pastor in Europe who she felt would help her obtain a new passport. Rev. Dave said he would contact him.

We approached her new contact with some apprehension and awaited his reply. Within a few days, Rev. Dave did receive an email from that pastor in Europe.

"Cindy is not mentally well," the man wrote. "She should not even *have* a passport, because it gets her in trouble when she travels. And presently, she was actually supposed to be in the United States getting help."

I felt depleted, disappointed, and sorry for her. Now what? How could we help someone who didn't feel they had a problem?

The next day, I prayed, *Father, I come to You this morning feeling bruised in my pride and ego, because I believed parts of Cindy's story and I now find she has taken reality and distorted it to the point where she is "hunted" in her own mind.*

I confessed my need to be *right* and how upset I got when I felt I'd been conned. Yet a part of me ached to help her in some way. She had a deep-rooted hurt that must have caused her to begin this fantasy.

My prayer continued. *Father, I desperately need something in Scripture that will help me to understand or know what action, if any, we are to take in Cindy's regard.*

Then, I read in James 5:16, *"The prayer of a righteous person has great power as it is working."* I believed the Lord was showing me that all I could do was pray for healing for her.

What came to mind next was something I had read during my spiritual journey, that the more we pray, the more power we have. But if we fail to pray, there is no power. I felt less responsible, knowing that all I could really do was pray, as all healing ultimately comes from the Lord.

Sadly, I now looked at Cindy through different eyes—from the possibility of her being semi-stable to definitely mentally ill.

Rev. Dave contacted her to let her know that he had heard from the pastor and asked if she could come in to see us. He knew that we would have to tell her that she needed more help than we were able to offer. But would she accept that help? Did she want to be healed, like the man at the pool Jesus met in John 5:6? Or would she choose to continue to live in her fantasy world?

When Cindy met with us, she was disappointed with the European pastor's response and that there would be no help from their end to get her a new passport. So she said she was prepared to go to the embassy in Ottawa instead.

Rev. Dave gave her the money she needed to pay for a renewed passport and a new copy of her birth certificate. Cindy was very grateful, but she again expressed concern over her safety. We prayed with her for the desired safety and for a sense of peace for her.

I had her on my mind as she prepared to go to her embassy. I prayed protection on her, both for her real and imaginary fears. I didn't know what *was* real or imagined, though, so I prayed, *Open the eyes of my heart, Lord.* Then God gave me the words of Psalm 46:5, which says, *"God will help her when morning dawns."* I felt peaceful.

Cindy came to the church after her visit to the embassy. She said that she had felt "threatened" and "treated like dirt" by the clerk and was now worried about her safety once again. She then swiftly switched from her fear and said that she wanted to join our weekly Bible study class. I told her that she was more than welcome to attend.

Surprisingly, she did show up at the Bible study group and I was very glad that one of our parishioners, a family therapist, was also in attendance. I prayed that the two of them would connect in some way. But Cindy didn't remain in the class long enough for that to happen.

In the meantime, she had asked me to send an email to a female contact in the United States, which I did. After a couple of weeks, she returned to ask for advice since she hadn't received a response from her American friend and felt this was telling her that her life was in danger once again. She asked if I would keep her new passport and other important papers so they wouldn't be at risk of being stolen in the women's shelter where she'd been staying.

We stored them in a locked file in the church office.

I was happy that she'd obtained her passport. Rev. Dave felt that she needed to be pastored into returning home to the United States.

Another thing I had been doing to assist Cindy was cashing her social security cheques for her, but the last one was returned. Cindy arrived elated because she had also received the new copy of her birth certificate. But when I had to tell her that I could no longer cash her cheques, as the last one had been returned, she got very upset and claimed that "they" had infiltrated and cut off another source of money.

I refused to be part of her paranoia.

"That's your perception, Cindy," I said. "I don't believe *they've* infiltrated *my* account. The bank just won't do double endorsements anymore because there is so much fraud."

She got upset and asked for her passport and documents back, saying that she'd moved to another room in the shelter and felt safer.

Rev. Dave and I met to talk about Cindy and how it had become more apparent just how paranoid she really was.

"People like her try to rope us into their fantasy by claiming to hear from God," he said. "After all, how could *we* as Christians go against what *God* says?"

We saw Cindy only a few times after she retrieved her documents. One day she requested to be allowed to sit quietly alone in one of the church rooms during daytime hours. I told her she could but that I would have to shift her around from time to time due to other people or groups having booked those rooms. I also told her that she would have to leave the building by 1:30 p.m. when our maintenance man locked the doors.

After a few Fridays of using various rooms, we then didn't see her for over a week. We never heard any word from her ever again. Perhaps she didn't like being shifted around. Or more sadly, she probably thought "they" had gotten to me and she was no longer safe at the church. I prayed for her mental health and healing from her own demons.

Joseph was another fragile, delusional fellow who needed mental and spiritual healing. He showed up at a special service we had titled Church on Its Knees. He started to pray out loud, as folks were encouraged to do, but he was *overly* prayerful to the point of domineering the prayer session. Others at the meeting felt uncomfortable, as some of his prayers were quite inappropriate. There were obvious mental health issues and the Clergy had to shut him down. He left quickly and those in attendance prayed for him.

We didn't see him again after that evening.

A young man, Charlie, once came in requesting to see a priest. I told him that all of the staff were in prayer time and asked what he needed.

"I'm confused about religion," he said.

I asked him if he could come back at eleven o'clock.

However, during prayer time I felt bad—and as we prayed, I felt that I should have let Rev. Dave tend to him, as his needs had been more important at that moment than the needs of the staff.

"Do you think there are mental issues?" asked Rev. Dave.

"Yes." Then I added, "It was his eyes."

I felt bad for judging him so quickly and silently prayed, *Father, is Your Holy Spirit leading me or is my own flesh judging him?*

Charlie was heavily on my mind during prayer time.

Then, around eleven o'clock, he did come back and Rev. Dave met with him.

"He is schizophrenic, on meds, and says God that doesn't love him," Rev. Dave later told me. He had tried to pray with Charlie. When he'd ended with "In the name of Jesus," Charlie, in his schizophrenic state, had said, "The devil is here. I have to go." With that, he promptly left!

Another time, a woman named Meg asked to use the church lounge for a few minutes. She ended up staying most of the morning and settled herself in, talking and laughing loudly to herself.

"They're watching us," she kept saying.

Finally I had to ask her to move along, since her ranting had become quite scary. As she was leaving, she handed me three long, threatening letters she had written to Beth and me. I stored them in our incident file in case there were further visits, but thankfully we never saw her again.

Peter was another troubled person who came into the parish office initially for food, which we provided. He was a tall, slender man with long, straggly hair. He started to arrive on a regular basis and was usually sitting on the laneway stairs when I arrived at 7:00 in the morning. I always told him he would have to wait until we opened the doors at 8:30, since I wasn't about to let anyone into the building until our maintenance man arrived. I sensed I needed to set boundaries with him when he started to hang around the church so frequently.

We as a church were able to meet his practical needs of food and a safe place, but Peter started to *live* in the church foyer, basically in and out from the moment the doors opened at 8:30 a.m. until closing time at 1:30 p.m.

One morning when I told him yet again that he was early and would have to sit and wait until we got the office rolling, he apologized for getting on my nerves. I felt bad and assured him he wasn't on my nerves... yet I still wouldn't get him his sandwich early. Setting boundaries was difficult with some of our street friends.

After a few months of Peter's regular visits, he still seemed pleasant enough, but he started to tell us that he was "hearing voices." He wanted me to call his doctor at the local mental health hospital, but I told him his doctor wouldn't talk to me because of patient confidentiality. If he really wanted it, we could take him to the clinic there, but he resisted that.

We knew we had to keep him in prayer with this new revelation of schizophrenia.

One day, I was just plain grumpy and Peter's incessant rambling and talking out loud to hear his own voice didn't help my mood. I tried to encourage him to go to one of the local ministries for breakfast instead of feeding him at the church every morning. I tried to avoid him, but I knew he had really come for food.

I felt guilty, so I fed him while praying to myself, *Father, help me to be moved with compassion instead of guilt and frustration.*

Peter continued to visit daily and started to become belligerent. One day he started yelling and swearing. I tried to calm him, but he wouldn't listen. My husband Bill, who was covering for our maintenance man, heard what was going on and came down the stairs toward the office. I was concerned that Bill would manhandle Peter, but instead he just stood there as a male presence for me.

Peter swore at him, me, and Beth, who was preparing to call 911.

Suddenly I yelled as loud as I could, "Peter, do you want a cup of tea?"

He stopped his rant and quietly replied, "Okay."

This shocked us all. He calmed right down, like a small child after a tantrum!

He stayed away for a few weeks and then came in yelling loudly, once again swearing and threatening us. I gave him a sandwich and he left.

Since I was planning to be away from the office the following two days, I told our maintenance man that if Peter came in with the same attitude, he should be asked to leave or the police would be called. I knew Peter would be upset, but he'd calm down in a month or so and be back.

On the days Beth and I were alone in the office, we kept the main church doors locked and prayed we'd have no trouble, especially from Peter. Thankfully, God helped us on those days, and to our knowledge no street friends knew we were alone.

Peter and other angry, lonely folks continued to be in my daily prayers throughout the remainder of my time at the church.

THE TRAVELLERS
They Just Want to Go Home

FROM TIME TO TIME, WE WOULD meet with people who were looking for help to get from one destination to another. Because of the limited rector's discretionary fund, it was important to really discern the need at hand. Some folks just wanted an opportunity to go to another town for a change of scenery—and if so, we usually didn't meet that request—while others, for whatever personal reason, had a genuine need to get to another place. Most of them had made an honest effort to get there on their own, perhaps by hitchhiking or working part-time at odd jobs along the way.

Our protocol was to always ask for identification and some proof for their reason to want to travel. If able, we would check out their story and contact someone at their desired location to try and verify the request. But sometimes we would just get a sense of knowing that they really needed to get to where they wanted to go and so we'd help them in their travelling.

Derrick initially came in looking for someone to talk to, so together we went into the main sanctuary of the church and sat in a pew. He told me he was desperate, that he was from the east coast and needed to get to a specific military base in Ontario to see his dad. He said that "some guy" at the base had put money into an account for him, but he wasn't able to access it.

He gave me his ID, his kids' ID, and his contact's phone number at the military base—and I called to verify the info. It turned out that his contact was legitimate and happened to be the base padre. He verified Derrick's story and said that he'd reimburse the church for the costs to send him to the military base.

I returned to Derrick and told him that we'd send him by bus to his destination. He was so grateful and told me that it had taken a lot of courage to walk in and ask. It certainly had!

Sadly, most of us tend to think that people in need have no pride, that they just ask and ask. But I've learned that they *do* have to swallow their pride, and it takes courage to do the asking.[9]

My adult daughter happened to be with me in the office on the day Derrick came in. It was good for her to hear our conversation, as it gave her a better understanding of street people's needs and the real work done at an inner-city church. It also gave her a newfound sense of compassion for all of God's needy people. God had a plan that day and she became part of it.

Derrick later called me from the bus terminal. The clerk was giving him a difficult time and didn't want to give him the ticket. I asked to speak to her, who it turned out was new at her job. I explained that the church had often sent letters to the bus depot and their accounting department had always accepted them in the past. I asked her to please check with them, which she did. Then she came back on the phone and assured me that Derrick would be given his ticket.

Leaving work that day, my daughter and I drove to the terminal. I wanted to make sure that Derrick had in fact received his ticket. As I was turning into the terminal, I saw him walking out. I honked my horn and he came over, smiling with his ticket in hand.

Thank You, Jesus, I silently prayed.

When I asked if he'd eaten, he said, "No. No money."

I knew he wouldn't be able to go eight more hours on the bus without food, so I gave him five dollars. It wasn't much, but then my daughter dug into her tote bag and gave him a candy bar she had brought along, as well as some cheese and cracker snacks.

"Goodbye and God bless," I said to Derrick before we departed.

As my daughter and I headed home, she said sadly, "I can't imagine being without *any* money or food at all and yet travelling all the way from the east coast."

---

[9] Forgive me, Father, for my assumptions and judgments at times.

I finished the journey home with a smile on my face and grati-tude. *Thank You, Father, for bringing Derrick to the church today. It was so good for my daughter to witness this encounter firsthand and grasp the need on our city streets.*

Three men came in together for bus tickets one day, and Rev. Dave happened to be there as I spoke with them. I thought I'd handled them well, demonstrating firm compassion.

But then I noticed Rev. Dave cringe a little when I told one of the men, who wanted to go to Kingston the following week, "We are not a travel agency. Either you go today or you'll have to come back and try again."

I had a lot to learn about firm compassion!

One especially memorable day, we had a young brother and sister drop in. They were both in their late teens and had visited other churches in the area with their request. They couldn't believe there was no help available for them. They had made their way to Ottawa from New Brunswick by bus-hopping.

Their dad had passed away two days prior, from cancer, and his funeral was to take place in Toronto at the end of the week. They needed a bus ticket to get the rest of the way there.

Rev. Dave happened to be in and asked them to come back with proper identification, since they had left their bags in a locker at the bus station.

When they returned with the proper paperwork, I asked, "Where are you from in New Brunswick?"

"Saint John," the young woman replied.

I told them I was originally from there as well. The young teens excitedly proceeded to tell me where they lived and about their life there. As I was very familiar with the area, Rev. Dave and I both felt they were sincere in their request. So we prepared a letter for the bus station to give them two one-way passes to Toronto.

After they left, my tears flowed for those precious teens.

Rev. Dave consoled, saying, "That's okay. Some can really move you. You'll learn to know when they're *not* sincere."

Another traveller was a hearing-impaired man. He was waiting in the foyer after our staff prayer time and handed me a note asking to go home to the Niagara area. I have a soft spot in my heart for the hearing-impaired, because my maternal grandparents had both lost their sense of hearing at young ages.

Because I had grown up close to my grandparents, I was able to communicate with this fellow in sign language. The clergy hadn't known about my hearing-impaired grandparents and were quite surprised when I signed to the young man.

Rev. Dave approved his bus ticket and the fellow was so excited that he hugged me and kissed my cheek! He then signed "Thank you" to Rev. Dave and I translated.

"You are welcome!" Rev. Dave yelled to him.

I laughed and said, "No matter how hard you yell, he can't hear you!"[10]

I silently prayed, *'Thank You, Jesus, for the opportunity to use another talent in Your service!*

Sadly, I've lost a lot of my ability to sign since my grandparents passed away many years ago. The newer American Sign Language (ASL) has replaced many of the signs I knew in my youth.

---

[10] I've seen this happen before in conversations with hearing-impaired people.

THE ANGRY AND EVIL
First Friendly, then Forceful

REV. DAVE HAD THE ABILITY TO look at some people and actually see a black cloud around them—to him, they looked scary. With me, I could see a hollowness, even "evil" sometimes, when I looked directly into their eyes. In prayer, I would ask, "Father God, how do we as good Christians really help these people without getting caught up in some of their mind games and without feeling resentful for the time we have to spend with them? How do we balance this *used* feeling we have at times with the desire to serve them as Jesus would have?"

I knew I didn't have the strength to be everything that some folks expected of me, nor did Rev. Dave, but God knew where and when we'd be able to really help. He would give us the strength and love to do it willingly.

When Rev. Dave announced he was going on a sabbatical, we began to realize that all the codependent street people were angry at him for going away. Apparently, many of them thought they wouldn't get the ongoing help they needed.

It was amazing what God had me learn in my first four years. The preparation had all been for His purposes, and my work had certainly not been routine! In the beginning of my work at the church, I had been naïve, but I was seldom shocked at anything I heard or saw anymore. Thanks to Rev. Dave's guidance, I was better equipped for this ministry.

The first time Jonathan came in, I recall a man of medium build with black hair and deep penetrating eyes that were very disconcerting when he glared at us. When he came to the church, he appeared suddenly. That first day, he was babbling about his girlfriend, then asked, "Is that thing for Grant this weekend?"

He was referring to a farewell party which had been planned for Grant, the person who had worked in the parish office before me. I had been told by some parishioners that he and Grant had been friends and that Jonathan wasn't happy that I had taken his friend's job.

"Yes, it is," I replied.

Jonathan pointed to the wall and motioned. "I told him when I die I'd put a plaque right here, and one for him. Death is real, you know. Death happens and shit happens, too."

Then he left as suddenly as he had appeared.

I took a deep breath. Then I had the feeling that I'd better share this with the woman who was setting up for the event. I took her aside and told her what Jonthan had said.

"Oh great, now we can both worry!" she replied. "I'll keep my eye out for him on Saturday."

I hoped she'd related this to the other volunteers as well, in case he did show up at the event.

Jonathan continued to visit from time to time, just lurking around, always sneakily. One minute he was here, then there, and always glaring with those scary eyes. He even gave our maintenance man the creeps.

This went on for a number of years and we eventually got used to his unexpected appearances.

One day, we learned that he had passed away. It was interesting to read the writeup about him in the local paper. He had also visited other churches in the area and was praised by them for having been "a gentle, loving soul." I was glad to read that, although my memories of him weren't as pleasant. It appeared I had been the target of his anger, having taken his friend's place in the parish office.

Another angry individual was Clark. He was a big fellow, and the first time I saw him he was rough-looking, like an ex-boxer. He had a huge black eye and had obviously been drinking.

Clark asked if the pastor was in and rambled on that he needed money for bus tickets and a place to lie down. It was about eleven in the morning.

"If you like, you may sleep on a pew at the back of the church," I told him. "But there's a service at noon, so I'll have to wake you then."

I pointed the way to the main sanctuary and he thanked me.

Then I thought of our altar guild lady, all alone in the vestry. If he saw the door open, I felt he might head toward it. Sure enough, I went into the church and found him with her in the chancel. I redirected him to a pew.

He was sweating profusely, said he felt sick, and asked if I had any water, soda, or milk. I got him a canned soft drink and again pointed to a pew where he could sleep. I was fairly calm throughout this, firm but polite.

Then I saw our maintenance man, Jack, and told him, "Clark has one hour to rest on the pew."

But Jack wanted to throw him out—and the next thing I knew they were both coming into the office area, arguing. Clark said he felt harassed.

"She made a mistake," Jack yelled. "You can't sleep here!"

Their voices were getting louder. As I was new to the position at the time, I realized that I had a situation on my hands.

"If I've made a judgment error here, I'm sorry," I said to Jack. "However, I did promise this gentleman that he could sleep for an hour—so I'll keep that promise this time."

Clark headed back into the sanctuary.

"It can only get worse," Jack argued with me. "It's not right. You're wrong! It isn't breaking a promise if you've been conned!"

Jack walked away, angry and upset.

I felt bad but thought of what Jesus said in Matthew 25:40: *"And the King will answer them, 'Truly, I say to you, as you did it to one of the least of these my brothers, you did it to me.'"*

43

I then telephoned one of our church wardens and pleaded for help, explaining the situation.

"There is no right or wrong here," she wisely said. "Just a difference of opinion between you and Jack."

She was okay with what I had done. We prayed over the phone for Clark, for Jack, and for us to be able to work out our differences.

Clark came down to the office, very restless and unsettled but polite. Then he said he was uncomfortable. Could I just give him five dollars for food? I told him that wasn't my normal practice, but I'd do it one time only to help.

Giving Clark the five dollars was worth it. I then silently prayed for everyone involved.

Jack and I talked afterward and both agreed that we'd just had a difference of opinion. The one thing I learned from this was to rely on God's strength and pray through every situation. The Holy Spirit got me through that one!

Clark came back three weeks later, and I must admit that I was a little nervous. He asked if he could come inside as he was freezing and his legs were cold. He wore thin trackpants and I noticed that he had another black eye.

"You can come in if you promise not to give our maintenance man a hard time like you did last time," I told him. "That makes me nervous."

"I promise."

He wanted to see the pastor, but Rev. Dave wasn't in. He asked for a blanket; I didn't have one, but I gave him a donated woollen coat to put over his legs and asked him to wait in the church where it was warmer.

Feeling nervous, I prayed for him, for Jack and for me and for peace between the three of us. I also prayed that Rev. Dave would return soon! I felt angry at myself for the fear I felt. I didn't feel that Clark would harm us, but I did fear another argument, even though this time he was sober.

When Rev. Dave arrived, I explained a little about Clark and his last visit. Rev. Dave commented that Jack had little use for street folk, which explained his strong negative reaction. I gave Rev. Dave my panic button, which he gladly took in case Clark got out of hand; he was big, strong, and obviously a scrapper.

Rev. Dave talked to him and found out that he was from the east coast but couldn't go back, since no one there wanted him to return. He also said he'd been barred from every hostel in Ottawa. He had no self-esteem, no food, and no money.

The end result of their conversation was that he wanted to go to Toronto, to start over. Rev. Dave decided that Clark really had nothing left in Ottawa, so he agreed to send him one-way by bus to Toronto. He also gave Clark his own lunch and drove him to the bus terminal. He called me from there to let me know that Clark was on his way.

Rev. Dave always had much wisdom and a big, caring heart!

Another day, a very angry man entered the office foyer. There was rage in his eyes and in his mannerisms. I prayed for protection, as I was all alone that day. In my morning prayer, I had symbolically put on the full armour of the Lord. (Ephesians 6:11–17).

I also realized that I'd forgotten my panic button at home! I prayed, affirming from Scripture the words of God: *"Do not be afraid, for those who are with us are more than those who are with them"* (2 Kings 6:16). Thankfully, the angry man left and I remained safe throughout the day.

When Darren came in to see Rev. Dave, he seemed to be a rather strange fellow. As I listened, their conversation grew louder and louder. Darren left the office yelling.

"I won't be back," he said. "Obviously I'm not good enough. I don't fit in!"

I know Rev. Dave was concerned, since he wasn't in the habit of making people feel like they weren't good enough.

Another difficult person almost attacked him on a Sunday because he had smiled at him during communion. The man had loudly said during the service, "What are you sneering at?"

Then there was Harry. I had just arrived at the office when two beat cops in their bright yellow police jackets entered the foyer. They wanted to talk to us about a guy we knew, Harry, specifically about his drug abuse. They explained that we needed to work together with the police to discourage Harry's actions to keep the general public safe. They also wanted us to help in encouraging him to stay at a local men's shelter.

"We're paid to be cynical, to do the research, to know them and be the 'bad' guys," one of the officers said.

Rev. Dave and I listened to what the officers had to say about Harry and other panhandlers in the area.

After they finished talking, Rev. Dave looked at me for feedback.

"Quite frankly, Harry frightens me," I said. "He can be very belligerent and nasty."

Rev. Dave then expressed that he was concerned about Rev. Jennifer's and my safety.

After much back and forth dialogue with the officers, it was decided that Rev. Dave would ask Harry to move on. He confessed to me that this was the part of the job he hated. I could feel his angst.

"Look," I said to the two policemen. "Harry doesn't like you fellows anyway. As you just told us, to him you're the 'bad' guys. So can we just tell him, 'Harry, we know the police are going to come and force you to move, so why don't you just go to the shelter?'"

The two officers agreed that we could let them be bad guys anytime we needed.

After they chased Harry, he came storming into the church thinking that Rev. Dave had called the police. One officer saw him re-enter the building, then came back in and told Harry that it had been local business owners calling them, not the priest.

Harry was extremely angry and heated, so Rev. Dave talked to him in a calming manner and he finally left.

Rev. Dave became concerned, though, because he was to be away from the church the next day. He was worried about Rev Jennifer and me and what might happen should Harry return. I reminded him that Bernie, our maintenance fellow who also happened to be a retired police officer, would be back from vacation.

We were all relieved about that, but thankfully Harry did not return.

Out my office window I saw a fellow in the church laneway. Bert appeared to be just standing talking to himself. I continued my work.

Later, I heard the church door open, but no one entered. I waited and prayed, *Lord, for whoever is walking in, may we be of some help.*

The door opened and closed several times, and each time I had this overwhelming sense of evil. I prayed for protection for us in the church and for the fellow outside. I could see him in the laneway mirror.

Eventually he came in and asked me if I would call a local Christian counselling service. I asked his name, and when he told me I realized he was the fellow who had asked for prayer in the church on Sunday. I had been told to probably expect him to drop in this week.

"Before I call the counselling service," I said, "I'll let Rev. Jennifer know you're here."

I dialled her extension, and thankfully Rev. Dave was with her as well. They took a long time coming to the front office as they discussed how best to deal with this individual. This left me to chat with him. He was *very* troubled.

"Something is attacking my feet and legs when I try to walk," he said. "Am I doing the right thing calling the counsellors?"

"Yes, you are. They are very good Christian counsellors and you've done the right thing by asking for prayer and coming back to the church."

From what I'd been told, Bert had been prepared to throw himself in front of a bus before he'd gone to ask for prayer on Sunday.

I prayed intensely as I waited for the two clergy. I needed Jesus to help so I wouldn't say the wrong thing and cause him more mental harm.

"You really know God," he said after a while. "I can tell."

"Yes, I do. He is a loving and gentle God and He loves you, too."

I kept wishing the clergy would hurry up!

Finally they came to the office and talked to him while I went into the sanctuary to do my daily routine.

Soon the two clergy and Bert came into the church and I heard the clergy encouraging Bert to take things one step at a time.

"Focus on Jesus with each step," they added.

I recall thinking how very inadequate I felt. This particular type of ministry in regard to demon possession was way out of my league.

Rev. Dave and Rev. Jennifer were able to calm Bert and they agreed to connect him with the Christian counsellors. When he left, they came into the office to debrief me about their conversation with this troubled man. Both felt he was schizophrenic, and Rev. Dave expressed his concern that he didn't want either Rev. Jennifer or me to be alone with him should he return.

But Bert never came back.

Another day, a woman telephoned seeking exorcism and deliverance. At that point, I was seldom shocked anymore about mental health and spiritual issues, so I suggested she come in and meet with a priest.

She showed up at our weekly healing service. Thankfully she wasn't disruptive to the others, but she was definitely demonized and in need of healing. She received much-needed prayer.

I arrived at the church one very cold morning to see someone sleeping in the side lane. After I'd gotten settled into my office, a very tall and broad-shouldered man with blondish hair and deep blue eyes entered. He introduced himself as Buddy. Initially he had a warm, broad smile, but as the weeks and months passed we saw a different side of him; he gradually became quite belligerent.

Buddy continued to sleep in the side lane of the church, tucked into a corner in spite of the intensely cold weather.

One morning the temperature reached minus forty degrees with the windchill. After exiting my car, I slowly approached his body wrapped tightly in a sleeping blanket, afraid that he was dead. But as I neared, I could see that he was breathing. His nose was red and the tip was white, an early indication of frostbite.

I gently called his name and told him that he had some frostbite and should get inside to a warm place. I felt compelled to give him some money for a hot breakfast so he could get out of the cold and bring up his body temperature.

As the weather changed from the winter cold to the spring rains, Buddy eventually started to sleep on the back ramp overnight. It had a sheltered roof, allowing him to remain warm and dry. The staff agreed to allow this, but we told him not to arrive until after the daily church activities had ended at 10:00 p.m.; he then needed to depart by 8:00 a.m., when our maintenance man arrived for the day.

Initially Buddy agreed to these terms, but soon he started to push the envelope—and our buttons!

One morning when I arrived, he was sleeping at the entrance to the back door ramp. I didn't want to wake him. Not out of kindness, but fear of his reaction since he was becoming more difficult to deal with. As I walked around to the front lane door, my blood was boiling. He was literally camping out on the back ramp and creating an unsightly mess, spreading out all his meagre possessions along with papers and food wrappers. As hard as I tried, I didn't feel very Christian toward him.

When Bernie arrived for work, he reminded Buddy to be all packed up and ready to leave by 8:00. But Buddy continued to ignore our directions, wouldn't pick up the stuff he had scattered, and rarely left the ramp until noon! He had become arrogant, and it was increasingly difficult for staff and others attending daily church events to enter through the back door.

Forgive my annoyance with Buddy and for losing my patience with him, I prayed daily. *Help me to show Christian love for all Your children. I just wish he wasn't so belligerent. I need Your grace, Lord.*

After several months of Buddy's refusal to listen to us, Rev. Dave asked me to proceed with calling the police to enforce a ban on Buddy after 8:00 a.m. Rev. Dave apologized to Bernie and me for having to deal with him.

I really felt sad. I didn't care if he slept on the back ramp in the cold and damp, but I understood that he needed to respect church space once the doors opened for the day. So I reluctantly called the police, who came and moved him along. Buddy was now banned from the church property.

A week later, I arrived to find him sleeping in the side laneway once again. I felt there was no point telling him he'd been banned and to leave, so I just called the police. I shook while I did this. Buddy was God's child, too, and my heart went out to him. But I had to enforce *our* boundaries.

Two officers arrived to move him along, but Buddy took his sweet old time.

After calling the police a couple of other times, we no longer saw him around the church. Interestingly, a few months later I happened to see Buddy sitting on a street corner while my husband and I were visiting a small town in the Muskoka area.

I decided it was best not to approach him!

Rod was another fellow who pushed my buttons. He was rude and crude and I became very angry with his demands.

One day I went to Rev. Dave's office to express this anger I was feeling. Rev. Dave saw a new side of me that day and was supportive. When I told him what a frustrating fellow Rod was, he found it all very funny and called me "human."

In our staff prayer time the next day, I confessed my anger and relayed to everyone there my morning Scripture lesson. The lesson said that Christians who are anything but gentle, who show no patience and little kindness, actually harm Christ's cause. We must follow Jesus's example and be tender, kind, and gentle in spirit.

This wasn't always easy and I knew God had a *lot* of work to do in me.

Ken was an aggressive man who came in demanding local bus transit tickets. When I told him we didn't give away during the summer months, he got very angry.

"I might as well just kill myself," he said. "I'll walk into the traffic right now and the church will be to blame! It will be on your head!"

Oh great, I thought.

I didn't relent to his threat, but I did pray hard for him as he stormed out.

A few days later, while we were hosting our yearly parishioners' meeting, Ken entered the church and asked for copies of the vestry documents. He got upset again when I explained that the documents were mailed out to members only. He made some very nasty comments about us not caring and not including him. I ignored his outburst, but Jim, our weekend maintenance man, stuck close by to watch him. Thankfully, Ken subsequently left without incident… before the official meeting began.

THE DEPRESSED
Internally Lonely

WE STAFF TRIED TO BRING AS much comfort as we could to the street people, but it seemed that the depression got some of them in its grip. When this happened, we found ourselves out of our realm of expertise. Again, the best we could offer was listening, showing compassion, prayer, and meeting practical needs.

God was testing my resolve to put others first and seek Him in the midst of noise and busyness. I was reminded in Scripture that the Lord tried to withdraw at times, but the crowds followed Him and He had compassion on them. I often thought that God must have gotten tired of my grumbling and complaining at times!

Marg was a very distraught, depressed woman who came in asking for the priest. As there was no priest available at that time, I asked if she wanted to talk. She did, so I suggested we go into the church sanctuary. She told me she hadn't been in a church in over four years, since her daughter's funeral. She shared tearfully that she had lost two daughters in separate car accidents.

My heart ached for her. She said she felt so alone, not having a job or any friends. She needed to talk because she felt she just wanted to die. She lacked spirit because all the feeling inside was gone. I listened and asked if she wanted to pray, but she said she didn't, that she already had and didn't feel that God had heard her.

She thanked me for listening and kept on talking.

I became a little fearful when our maintenance man left the building because Marg talked about how angry she was and how she just wanted to lash out at people. I wished I'd brought my panic button into the church. I silently prayed for protection.

As we talked, suddenly she smiled and her face lit up! I told her she had a beautiful smile and that she should make an effort to smile more often. She said she hadn't smiled in a long time.

We talked about guilt and God's forgiveness and the peace that comes when we unburden ourselves to God and surrender to Jesus. She said she'd done so much wrong in her life that she didn't feel God could *ever* forgive her. I told her that I personally had a very colourful past, but He had forgiven me and that I'd only been a Christian for two years at that point. I *knew* He worked miracles!

Once again I asked, "May I pray for you?"

She nodded.

As I prayed, she cried softly. Then, after our prayer time, she felt embarrassed for crying. I told her not to be embarrassed; the tears meant that the Holy Spirit was moving in her, that God was nudging her and it was a good sign. I gave her the name of a contact at a local Christian counselling service and invited her back anytime.

Donna was another woman who was depressed. She dropped into the church one day during her lunch hour and told me that she always received drives into the city early in the morning even though she didn't start work until 8:30 a.m. She often got lonely during her wait and asked if the church was open during those hours, so she could come in, sit, and pray quietly before her workday began.

She sounded so fragile, making me think about how the clergy had recently been talking about opening the church early for people in need of quiet before work. I sensed that this was God's timing, so I told Donna the doors would be open as soon as I arrived at 7:00 a.m. the following day.

The next morning, I turned on a few soft lights and waited in prayer at the back of the sanctuary. I heard the main door open and then heard her step inside.

"It's so good to be here," Donna said quietly.

I let her soak in the peaceful atmosphere for a few minutes, then I felt led to speak to her out of politeness. She was chatty and expressed her loneliness, having recently lost some close loved ones.

She seemed to be a gentle person, but she told me she was hurting from the rejection of her adoptive family, and more recently the rejection of a co-worker. After listening a while, I suggested she walk around the sanctuary, feel at home, and pray. However, it was obvious that she just wanted to talk. I listened—with a little resentment, shamefully, in losing my own quiet time—and she stayed until it was time to go to work. She told me she was grateful for the time we had shared, and we hugged goodbye.

Before starting my own workday, I read my daily inspiration which reminded me that I was to give of myself and share with others what I wanted to keep to myself. I realized that today I was meant to share my quiet time with someone else.

Instantly I felt convicted about my thoughts of resentment over having lost my own quiet time that morning!

Forgive me, Lord, I prayed. *Your will be done, not mine.*

Another day, I received a distress call from an elderly lady who was in a panic. I was having a difficult time trying to understand what she was saying, as she was anxious and hyperventilating. I calmly listened, really wanting to understand what she was trying to express.

When she grew silent, I quietly told her that it would be best for her to speak to a professional counsellor. I gave her the number for the local Christian counselling service. I prayed she would contact them and be okay.

A couple of days later, I received a call from their executive director telling me that they had been able to help her. Thank You, Jesus!

THE ONE-TIMERS
Just Passing Through

AFTER A COUPLE OF YEARS WORKING at the parish, I found that I was able to remain much calmer in the midst of the noise, even on hectic days. When I'd started the job, I had really needed to get used to so much activity. I had always been an introvert, yet now I was expected to work with several extroverts!

Eventually I knew I'd finally reached a point of being able to accept the noise and disruptions at Saint G's. I was able to honestly pray, *Thank You for the privilege of serving You in this place.* I'd also taken to heart what Rev. Dave always said: "Prayer is the real work." Prayer really is a large part of what we did at Saint G's—prayer for so many folks, parishioners, and street friends from different walks of life.

Rev. Dave once asked, "Do you suppose they need administrators in heaven?" I laughingly replied, "I certainly hope not; I'm looking forward to that promised eternal peace!"

In reality, the work we did was for the Lord only. We needed to remain steadfast to ensure that nothing we did would be in vain.

I kept hearing the word compassion. As I mentioned earlier, Jesus always had compassion for people, in spite of the multitudes seeking His help. He always took the time to listen. Then He purposely made time to get away by Himself to talk to the Father, hear from Him, listen, refresh and renew I lis inner spirit. We all need to be refreshed from time to time.

Many people who visited the church were one-timers. They came to us for a specific need on a particular day and we never saw them again. One example was a misguided drunk who showed up at our Alpha™ course one evening. The church was filled with about seventy-five participants and course leaders. I personally felt the inebriated fellow didn't belong, but he stayed.

Forgive me, God, for my feeling that he doesn't belong, I prayed. *Maybe You felt he does.*

I had a lot to learn about street ministry.

An Indigenous lady came knocking on the door one day, and it was obvious she had very recently suffered a bad beating. But she insisted it had happened the previous week. She told me that some street gals had jumped her.

However, later that same day, she told one of our wardens that her partner had abused her. Whatever happened, she was in rough shape! We gave her some supplies and when she left we prayed for all our street friends, especially for the women alone out there.

Another day while at work, I saw through the office window an older woman crumpled in the laneway. One of our parishioners rushed in and asked me to call 911. I did—but I did so reluctantly, in case the woman was only drunk and uninjured.

As we waited for the ambulance, the parishioner and I sat together in the corner of the lobby, praying for her. This particular parishioner had a reputation for being a powerful prayer warrior and it was beautiful to hear and feel the words of compassion she had for this poor woman. I prayed not only for the woman but for those responding to the 911 call, that they would treat her with care and the compassion.

"I'm glad you said that," the parishioner said. She then told me a story of how she had once witnessed two police officers roughing up one of the street women.[11] In that case, she herself had stepped in to assist the troubled woman.

I received a call from a troubled young man who said his name was Otis. He told me that he had to get to England for his

---

[11] I know some of our law enforcement folk have a hard time dealing with street people, but we all need compassion, which isn't always easy to demonstrate.

grandfather's funeral. I explained that he would need to have proper identification before we could discern whether we could help, but he didn't have any ID and hung up the phone.

He called back the following week. This time he said that it was his father's body that was still waiting for burial. Knowing that his story had changed, I told him there was nothing we could do for him.

When an older fellow entered in tears, he explained that all his clothes had been in a bag and someone had stolen it. I called the Salvation Army and found out that he could get a voucher there with proper ID to replace his clothes. I just hoped he had some ID! He was crying as he left and I thought about the fact that everything he owned had probably been in that bag.

A young man named Jay walked into the church sanctuary while the clergy and I were discussing plans for an upcoming event. He said that he needed financial and emotional help. I sensed that he preferred to talk to a priest, so I went back to my office and left him alone with our two clergy.

The clergy shared afterwards that Jay had told them he owed drug money, about a hundred dollars, and needed help as his family was now being threatened. He had seemed genuinely fearful.

After much debate, chatting, and verification, Rev. Dave decided to give him fifty dollars if he would agree to go to detox. Apparently that was a tough decision for him to make. His whole conversation with the clergy lasted one and a half hours as they tried to get him settled and fed.

Before I left for the day, the two clergy and I joined in prayer for Jay as he left with the fifty dollars. We prayed for his safety, his health, and for the Holy Spirit to convict his conscience.

The agreement was that Jay would come back the next morning. But he didn't return.

"We got taken," Rev. Dave said.

I know this compassionate priest felt badly. "It's only money," I said. "And it's on Jay's conscience now."

We added his name to our ongoing prayer list.

Another older fellow came in wanting to get home to Halifax. I recognized him, knew he had been in before, and was sure he'd previously been given a ticket. We have a one-time only policy.

When I looked back on my records, I saw that he had indeed received a ticket once before. But his new story about a family funeral checked out, so we sent him home, again with the understanding that he'd have to cover his own fare back. He understood. My heart ached for him.

One day, a strange woman came in and left a letter for Rev. Jennifer. The letter was eerie and troubling, and we soon found out that the woman lived in a local woman's shelter and that she had written similar letters to other female clergy in the area.

When a young woman named Chrissie came in very distraught, we talked and she let me pray with her. She reminded me of myself twenty-five years younger, because she was a single mom strapped financially and afraid.

In praying for others, I found that I needed to really listen and rely on God more and more each day. I also learned that by sharing part of my own story, I could help someone else in the same situation to know they weren't alone in their journey.

Some weeks were much busier than others. One particular week, we dealt with a mentally disturbed couple. The man came in talking about sex while the woman talked about holiness and love. Then a different fellow came in ranting that he hated feminists and, according to him, all women were feminists. Thankfully, he only came in the one time! We also met an ex-con who came in for food and clothes. Another guy wanted just a cup of cold water; I was instantly reminded of the verse in Matthew 10 which speaks of the simple gesture of giving a cup of cold water to someone shows that we are His disciple.

Another time, a very perverted fellow came by to talk to one of our volunteers. The volunteer said she felt dirty after their discussion, so we prayed for God to help her feel cleansed and renewed in Him. The fellow called back twice asking for her. We knew we'd have to monitor him if he continued to come back, but thankfully he didn't.

Then there was a young man who walked in with an older, obese man. The young man was asking us to pay his rent. I felt sad, thinking that he was just a kid. I wasn't getting a good feeling about his older companion, and thankfully Rev. Dave met with them and was practical and comforting.

Other one-timers included a woman from Romania who walked in asking for prayer, so Rev. Dave and I prayed with her. Then an *extremely* disoriented Asian came in. I felt nervous as I tried to discern his needs. I then asked Rev. Dave to talk to him, but he couldn't clarify what the problem was either. Sadly, we suspected this man was high on drugs. I made him a sandwich, which he quickly devoured. Jim sat with him for a while until he calmed down so Rev. Dave could return to his own pressing work.

Ricky was another one-time fellow who told us that he had walked from Thunder Bay and that it had taken him forty-four days. He wasn't well, very thin, and shaking. He had a bed waiting for him at a detox centre in Cornwall and gave us the name and number of his intake worker so we could verify this. Her name was Faith, which made me smile. How appropriate! We gave him a bus ticket to Cornwall to get the help he needed.

Another needy individual also wanted a bus ticket, this time to Moncton, New Brunswick. Rev. Dave spoke with him but didn't give him the desired ticket letter immediately. Rev. Dave did ask that he come back the following week after we were able to check how much was left in his discretionary fund at year-end. The fellow didn't return.

One particular Sunday while waiting for the service to start, I had a long-lost cousin on my mind. Then a tall straggly-haired, bearded guy came in and sat in one of the front pews. He was deemed a concern for our wardens, who kept a close eye on him during the service.

Out of the blue, I sensed God speak to my spirit, *"What if he were your long-lost relative?"* Convicted, I had to admit that I wouldn't be as anxious to connect with him.

As I sat in church with my eyes on this stranger and my mind on my relative, God showed me that I only wanted "perfect" people to get close to me, not the mentally ill or disenfranchised. It was painful to realize this side of my character.

Father, help me to lovingly accept all of Your precious children and not judge by appearance as I so often do, I prayed. *Help me to love those whom society has labelled "unlovable." Help me to love as You love.*

By far the best thing that happened was when we saved a life. A man dropped in for prayer and said he had been planning to commit suicide, but he called back later to say that he was safe and feeling much better. Praise the Lord!

When working in a church, especially in street ministry, you usually never know if you've really helped someone or not, so it's rewarding and encouraging when God allows us to hear some good news. He is the true Healer and we are blessed to be His hands and feet for others.

There Has to Be More to Life than This

AS A CHRISTIAN CHURCH BODY, WE knew that our biggest calling was to make disciples. The people mentioned in this section were those who were genuinely seeking *something more*. It was a privilege to pray with these people and be able to steer them in the direction of a personal relationship with Jesus.

Some days in the parish office were very humbling and I often thanked God for the ministry and blessing of seeing Jesus work in people's lives. It was a privilege for us at the church to be used by God as encouragers to others, to help them seek His face more deeply and for them to begin to hear Him speak into their lives.

We had to be careful to keep Jesus as the central focus, and to be equipped to do so we, as staff in His service, all needed to spend more time with Him in quiet ourselves. In our weekly staff meetings, we often prayed for wisdom and clarity and for Him to help us be His light in the dark.

I came to accept that interruptions were actually opportunities to know and show His grace. We all knew it was important to be in prayer with Him and available for Him when He called.

A man named Paul popped in one day to chat. Initially it was just small talk, but I could tell that he wanted to get into a deeper conversation, as he mentioned his on-again/off-again desire for church.

He asked if we were high or low Anglican.

"Low," I said. "But it doesn't matter, Paul. We have to let go of the differences in our dogmas. The bottom line is whether are we believers in Jesus Christ. *That* is the sign of a Christian. It's not about our religious practices or various buildings."

He replied, "It helps to talk to a Christian. I hope by some turn of fate you are able to meet my mother. You're a lot alike."

Rev. Dave asked me afterward if Paul had given me any trouble.

"Not at all," I told him.

He added that Paul had once hugged a female parishioner very inappropriately and it had made her feel uncomfortable.

"I trust eyes, and at one point I was feeling uncomfortable with his ogling," I told him. "Then I happened to mention to Paul that I was a grandmother. Suddenly, he backed off and said that I reminded him of his mother."

Rev. Dave and I both laughed at how my grandmother comment seemed to have put Paul in his place!

Another seeker, Ranvir, an East Indian gentleman, had seen the healing service signs outside the church and wanted to talk to the priest. He needed answers about healing and hadn't realized our particular church was "into that."

Ranvir had a Hindu background, was quiet and articulate, and told me he had a recently diagnosed heart condition. He needed to talk, and I offered to listen. He was on his way to the doctor's office but asked if he could come back the next day. I really wished someone else would be with me to pray with him.

All evening, I thought about the next day's meeting. What could I possibly say to help my new Hindu friend? I searched out all references to healing in my concordance and highlighted several Bible passages.

The next day, I was somewhat anxious anticipating Ranvir's return. I asked God to fill me with His Holy Spirit and give me the words to say to him.

Ranvir arrived around eleven o'clock. His request was that he wanted a "healer" to pray with on a weekly basis. As we talked, he totally opened up—to his surprise and mine. I tried to just listen and give him the space to talk freely. I found that I was more helpful when

I didn't try to plan what to say, but instead just really listened, prayed quietly, and hopefully spoke to him from the heart, with the Spirit's leading.

He told me that he was sixty-two, living alone now, and that his heart was bad. He was afraid and needed support. He had the medical side taken care of, but also wanted some help on the spiritual side and again expressed that he really felt he needed to pray with a "healer." Not considering myself a healer, I talked about my beliefs and how God heals today through Jesus and the Holy Spirit. He asked if I knew of anyone who had been healed.

"I do," I told him. "I know a lady who was healed of breast cancer, and another from leukemia."

I then shared about having had a relationship with Jesus myself for only two years, and about learning more about Jesus's healing powers since working at the church.

"Healing is more than physical," I said. "It is emotional and spiritual as well."

He understood. "I'm not looking for a dramatic evangelical or broccoli-eating meditator, but rather just a quiet layperson with whom I can pray weekly."

I told him that he could come to Saint G's anytime, but he was concerned about taking me away from my work. I assured him that praying was *part* of the work and that I knew Rev. Dave would be happy to meet with him as well.

Ranvir and I prayed quietly in the chancel. I just prayed what I believed the Spirit led me to say, while in my mind asking God to help me say the *right* words. We spent a very fast hour together and he thanked me after. I loaned him an Alpha™ course book called *Questions of Life*[12] and encouraged him to read the section entitled "Does God Heal Today?" Although I secretly hoped he'd read the whole book!

Ranvir came back a few days later to return the book, which he *had* read in its entirety. He asked about the course's start date as he was interested in participating. He admitted that he was a loner and

---

[12] Nicky Gumbel, *Questions of Life* (Colorado Springs, CO: Cook Ministry Resources, 1996).

not used to being around a lot of people, but he knew he needed to connect so he could build a support group.

He told me that he regularly attended our city's local Heart Institute and the doctors had asked him who they should contact, i.e. a spiritual person or priest. He told them he had no one but asked if he could refer them to me if he needed prayer at any time while in hospital. I told him he could give my name as a friend, but I encouraged him to come and meet Rev. Dave so that he'd have a priest as needed. He knew he had to take that step and said he'd come to our healing service that evening.

I talked to Rev. Dave about Ranvir, giving him the background info and letting him know to possibly expect him at the weekly healing service.

The next day, Rev. Dave told me that Ranvir had indeed attended. He believed it was divine guidance as there had been only a handful of others present and Ranvir had received the total undivided attention of the healing team, as well as much prayer from them.

Rev. Dave also found Ranvir to be articulate and definitely seeking, so he spoke to his heart about Jesus. When Ranvir asked if the reverend knew any healers, Rev. Dave replied, "The soul needs as much healing as the heart."

Later Rev. Dave solemnly said to me, "I didn't want to panic him, but this may be God's way of saying 'You don't have much time. Get saved now!'"

Ranvir had walked past Saint G's for fifteen years and never noticed the sign about healing, and I was so thankful that he'd come in and had the opportunity to talk and also receive healing prayer. Ranvir requested to come every Wednesday for prayer and Rev. Dave had no hesitation at all.

He continued to come for a few Wednesdays, and then we didn't see him again. I had to trust that he'd received the help he needed and would be well, both physically and spiritually.

Another drop-in who came for prayer was Bobby. He was about to have surgery to remove a brain tumour, so Rev. Dave took him into the church and the two of us prayed with him.

A few weeks later, Bobby came back to thank us for our prayers. During the surgery, the doctors had removed a large tumour from the front part of his brain.[13]

Rev. Dave asked if we could prayer with him again and hoped he wouldn't feel uncomfortable.

"I've never had a church connection," Bobby replied, "but prayer won't make me feel uncomfortable."

Rev. Dave prayed for continued physical healing and also for Bobby's spiritual healing.

I arrived at the church early one morning to find a couple of people tucked into an outside corner, asleep with some of their clothes hanging on the stair rails.

"Good morning, folks," I greeted them. "Time to get up."

Our church rule was that our overnight guests were to move on once our day began.

These are God's children, I thought. *He loves them. They are lost and need Him.*

I also prayed that I could see them from God's perspective, not mine.

The couple, Carl and Jan were both in their thirties. Carl was short and stout with black hair and dark eyes. He was missing a few teeth. Jan was petite and slender, with long dark hair and pretty eyes. They both had nice smiles. They were friendly and soon packed up their stuff and headed on their way.

We were to see a lot more of them over the next few months. Ministering to them and their needs proved to be one of my most memorable times at the church, filled with profound joy and then ultimately much sadness.

After a few daily visits, I wondered how I could show Jesus's love for them. I confessed to the Lord that I was somewhat afraid of them and didn't really trust them. I knew we'd need time to build up trust on both sides, me for them and them for me.

Initially I found Carl to be filled with deep anger, as he would rage about the unfairness of life. Jan sadly seemed to be a pathetic druggie. I really didn't see much hope in them. At first I saw them only as "takers," always in to visit and wanting something.

---

[13] Bobby went on to have an amazing recovery.

I asked Jesus to help me to see them with His eyes, with His compassion, and to help me love them as He loved them. I wanted to look at them not as a *problem*, but as a *purpose*. I didn't want to be a fixer but rather a caring, compassionate person toward them.

As I lay in bed one morning, thinking about Carl and Jan, I prayed for them. Then a thought came to me: *Why don't I tell them that I awoke thinking of them and prayed for them? I'll invite them into the chancel on their next visit, along with Beth, and we'll take the time to really listen and hear their story, if they're willing to share it.*

I had the sense that the Holy Spirit had lain this course of action on my heart.

As I arrived for the Sunday service, I was surprised to see Carl and Jan sitting at the back of the church. I asked if I could join them in the pew. I could see that they were being emotionally touched by the worship, so I encouraged them to go to one of the prayer stations after the service. Since I had a couple of duties to attend to, I said my goodbyes and left them to enjoy the hospitality time of coffee and sweets.

Arriving at work midweek, I saw Carl and Jan sleeping in their usual corner. They told me that neither of them had been feeling very well. I told them they could stay a while, and then I went into the early Wednesday morning service and silently prayed for them.

After the service, I asked Jan how she was doing.

"Not well," she replied. "No job. Frustrated."

I found myself asking if she'd gone for prayer on Sunday. She said that she hadn't been able to go, as it would have been too embarrassing. I'd been in that same situation years ago, so I understood.

She started to cry and I asked if I could pray with her right then.

Rev. Jennifer was close by, so I asked Jan if it was okay for her to join us. She agreed, and with Jan's permission I shared with Rev. Jennifer the issue of her lacking a job. We prayed over her.

Then I said to both Jan and Carl, "Come on, let's go to breakfast." It was our custom that everyone attending the early morning service would go out for breakfast together afterward.

Jan started to cry and I hugged her.

"Thank you," she whispered, hugging me back.

Carl and Jan continued to sleep at the church nightly, tucked into the laneway corner. But after a staff meeting discussion on boundaries one day, I had to talk to them and lay down some ground rules. They could sleep in the building's cubbyhole, but they couldn't arrive until after 10:00 p.m., and they would have to be packed up by 8:00 a.m. and gone for the day. I asked them if they understood and agreed. They nodded.

Then they asked for a signed paper that gave them permission to sleep in the laneway.

"We're not going to do that," I said. "I've told you what the church is willing to allow. By the way, the staff and clergy are praying for you every day, because God wants your spiritual needs to be met, not just your practical ones."

After a couple of months of Carl and Jan being at the church, it became obvious that we were building up a nice level of trust. Not only were they considerate of our church rules, but we were delighted to see them attending service most Sundays.

Then one day Carl told me, "We have a problem. It's embarrassing."

Beth and I invited them into the chancel to listen—and as we listened, I realized that we were now seeing this couple through Jesus's eyes. They both cried as they talked, holding each other's hands in mutual support. They admitted to abusing drugs and having other issues. They asked for help. Jan also confessed that because of her personal lifestyle, she had lost custody of her young daughter.

I let them know that this willingness to share their story was a *very* brave step for them and an answer to our prayers. We knew that Jesus had brought them here and wanted them to be healed and whole. I assured them that He loved them very much and that we as the church would try to get them the help they were seeking.

Then Beth and I prayed with thanksgiving for their willingness to be healed and assured them of God's love and protection for them. They had a long way to go from the street to healing, but we knew that nothing is impossible with God!

We hugged them after our time together. All of us were in tears.

Beth and I hugged each other when we got back into the office. This is what it was all about! This was the *real* work at our church, God Himself in action, bringing healing, wholeness, and salvation through Christ's love.

I called Rev. Jennifer. After briefing her on Carl and Jan's issues, she agreed that they should go through short-term Christian counselling. I went home exhausted, but in a warm and fulfilling way.

When Rev. Dave arrived back from holidays, I brought him up to speed on Carl and Jan. He decided that they needed to begin with a session or two with him before they were sent to the counselling service. He wanted to do his own assessment first, and rightly so.

I'd seen a woman speak on the television show *Crossroads.* She had shared her life story and written a book: *Betrayal: The Deepest Cut.*[14] I purchased the book, and reading her story gave me hope for Carl and Jan.

As I read, I sensed God tell me to give the book to Jan.

This may be good for her, I thought. And in other places, *She'll relate to this.* I didn't want to depress her, but rather give her hope for healing.

Then I thought, *This isn't up to me to judge. God pressed it on my heart to give it to her. He has His reasons.*

I relayed the message to Carl and Jan that they would have their first session with Rev. Dave. They were okay with that and said they were happy that the wheels were in motion. They also assured us that they had stayed clean.

I continued to pray for them. *One day at a time, Lord Jesus. Help them.*

A few days later, they arrived at the church excited as they'd just gotten the keys to a new rental room. Carl had fought for it and got it! They were both elated about their new space, but Jan was a little sad as a planned visit with her daughter had been cut short.

"One day at a time," I told her.

I then gave Jan the book and explained that the author's personal story may give her inspiration and hope. She cried and gave me a big hug.

---

[14] Carol Kornacki, *Betrayal: The Deepest Cut* (Lake Mary, FL: Creation House, 2007).

Carl and Jan moved into their new place and were finally dry and comfy. When they came into the church a couple of days later, they both seemed much happier.

"We have no light," Jan told me, "so I read the book you gave me with the fridge door open!"

I was glad she'd read the book, but also delighted to know that they had a fridge and also their own shower.

After a few weeks of living in their new place, they came in again, this time excited that Jan's ex had given them both permission to take her young daughter to the local Santa Claus parade. They asked if they could have ten dollars to buy a disposable camera to take pictures. I gave it to her as a one-time-only gift and asked her to be sure to show us the photos.

I hoped and prayed this visit would encourage them to stay clean for future access to her child.

They attended the early Sunday service that week and told me all about the parade the day before and the time they had shared with her daughter. They were elated!

Thank You, Jesus, I silently prayed.

Carl and Jan met again with Rev. Dave, who gave them some homework and made plans to meet them separately. He believed that the Holy Spirit was working in their lives.

When they showed us a picture of Jan with her daughter, I offered to have it enlarged. My husband kindly did that for her.

One day Jan came in to visit alone and asked if I could get a copy of the poem, *Footprints in the Sand* by Mary Fishback Powers.

"Carl has had such a rough life," she said. "I want him to read it."

With the help of the internet, I was able to obtain a copy for her. Jan said she subsequently read it to Carl and the words had deeply touched him.

Sadly, for reasons not shared with us, they had to leave the room they had been staying in and instead move into the YMCA. This was more expensive than their former room, but fortunately Carl had started working for a temporary labour agency and was able to cover the rent. Still, we prayed that they would find a more affordable place again soon.

As it was Christmas, I wanted to give them something just from me. Over the months, we had developed a bond and I genuinely thought of them as friends.

I knew they were in need, as Carl came in one day asking for butter.

"No butter, but I do have something for the both of you," I said. "A Christmas gift to you from me."

I felt the timing was right and gave them a gift certificate to a local grocery store. They hugged me and Carl said he had goose-bumps.

I had them as well.

Off they went saying they were going to get some good food.

Lord, a gift is a gift, I thought. *Help me not to wonder how they will spend it. I do pray they eat well.*

Within a couple of months, Carl and Jan had fallen behind on their payments at the YMCA and I got on the phone a few times with someone who worked there. The bottom line was that they could stay and pay when their cheque came in.

"Praise the Lord," I whispered.

I reiterated to Carl that he needed to pay the rent as soon as he got his cheque, which thankfully he did.

Jan called one day and sounded awful. I hoped she wasn't falling back into her old ways of using drugs now that she was alone at home all day while Carl was out working. I continued to pray for them and the church helped them as we were able. I prayed that God would use this time to change their hearts and lives.

I didn't usually answer the church phone on Sunday mornings, but I did one particular day and heard a message from Carl. He and Jan wanted to get a ride to the service. I knew they liked the quieter 8:30 service, but it was now 10:00. I felt in my heart that it was God's prompting for me to have checked the phone messages—so I'd better not ignore it!

I called their number at the Y. Jan answered and told me they still wanted to go to church, so I asked if they could be ready in five minutes. I then drove down the few blocks to get them.

When I arrived, they were friendly and looked good. They told me they had changed rooms and secured one that was better and much warmer.

We arrived at church in time. They sat at the back, seemingly enjoying the service and the hospitality time after. I knew they were hungry, since they filled up on cookies. But that wouldn't satisfy them for long.

I prayed for guidance. I didn't feel *anyone* should go hungry, not with all the food we have access to in Canada. The stores were full, yet these two people were empty. What could I do?

When I got home after church, I prepared a stew for supper and thought about Carl and Jan. My heart was troubled. I knew I had to give them another gift certificate for food.

Jan called one morning and told me that Carl was at work. Her speech sounded slurred and I wondered if she was high.

"No," she replied when I asked. "Just tired and crying all the time."

I worried that she'd slide back into old habits, continuing to be alone with no real purpose while Carl worked. She seemed so wrapped up in him, so dependent, so lost.

I asked if I could pray with her.

"When?" she asked.

"Right now, over the phone."

"What do I do?"

"Just listen, Jan."

As I prayed for her, she sobbed heavily. I knew God was doing something in her life, yet Jan was seemingly becoming more fragile.

Beth and I prayed together after I got off the phone.

After work, I took some work boots to the Y to give Carl. Jan was supposed to meet me outside at 3:15, but she didn't show, so I headed home.

I got a message on the church phone the next morning from her. In it, she said that she'd waited until 3:30. But I wondered, where? My concerns for her were deepening.

Later the same day, Rev. Dave answered the phone and heard Carl's voice asking for fifty dollars. Rev. Dave talked to him for a while and then delivered the money.

A few more weeks passed and Carl and Jan let us know that they had gotten settled into a new place farther away from the church. We didn't see them as often after that, but they did keep in touch by phone from time to time.

One Monday morning, I looked at the online obituaries, as was part of my daily routine to learn if any former parishioners had passed. I was shocked and saddened to see Jan's obit! My heart sank and tears welled up in my eyes.

Immediately I sensed that she had died from suicide or drug overdose. Yet in front of me was a very pretty picture of her in better days.

In my prayers this particular morning, I had prayed for her and Carl as usual and had a sense that they had split. As I read her obituary, I realized that they were now *permanently* split. My heart ached for her, her family, and especially her little girl. And of course Carl. There was no mention of him in the obituary. I wondered about him and prayed.

I called Bernie into the office to show him the obit notice. He too was shocked and upset.

I found I wasn't able to function well all day. I kept wondering, *Why did this happen? Did we make a difference in her life, even a little?* I was grateful for having known her and so sad for this tragic ending.

When Rev. Dave came in, he too was shocked and we prayed together. He shared with me an excerpt from Isaiah 58, which he had read earlier in the morning. It talked about ministering to God's needy people and how He honours that.

I had to cut him short, or I would have wept even more.

The phone rang on Friday later that week, and it was Carl. He was upset and crying. He told me that he was in a psychiatric ward at one of our local hospitals.

"Did you hear?" he asked. "Why did she do it? Why now, when we've been doing so well and got clean? We were on our feet. I can't live without her."

He rambled on about being lonely, having no cigarettes, and needing help. His words were tugging at my heartstrings and I wanted to run to the hospital with cigarettes in hand and to hug him in his loneliness and desperation.

We talked for fifteen minutes, and during this time he told me that Jan had jumped in front of a train. The story checked out as I later searched the local paper's web archive. He said that she'd gone out for a pack of cigarettes that morning, a Saturday, and then the police had come to their door with the tragic news. Carl relayed that he had apparently uttered death threats to their landlady, so the police took him to the psyche ward.

When Carl finished talking and we hung up, I called Rev. Dave, needing advice and wisdom. He was meeting with one of his clergy friends, Rev. Archie, and I relayed Carl's request about being lonely and needing cigarettes.

"Don't go," Rev. Dave said firmly.

I heeded that advice and instead went home. I felt empty, wondering if we'd made a difference in their lives at all.

I thought of Jan all week. Her death was so sad and difficult to accept. Why had she done it? What would happen to Carl now?

At the Sunday service, I had to decline being on prayer team. I just wasn't in the right frame of mind.

Rev. Dave's friend Rev. Archie came over to me after the service, gave me a hug, and asked, "How are you?"

I thanked him and said, "I needed a hug. It was a rough Friday after Carl's call."

I woke in the night with anxiety over Carl and his emotional state. Feeling overwhelmed, I prayed, *"I can do all things through him who strengthens me"* (Philippians 4:13).

Rev. Dave had told me not to take on Carl by myself, and I knew I needed to listen to his wisdom. Yet at the same time I worried that Carl was calling out to me and we were doing nothing. I was also concerned that he might take his own life when he was released from the psyche ward. Then I'd wondered even more, *'Where have we helped?'* This weighed heavily on my heart.

I found myself praying, *Father, forgive me for trying to take this all on my own shoulders. I pray that Carl is getting the medical, emotional, and mental help he needs. He is exactly where he needs to be—in professional care. I am not God!*

I continued to pray for Carl and asked others on our prayer team to do so as well. I prayed a chaplain would visit him at the hospital and pray with him. I prayed that if/when he called me, I would hear the Holy Spirit's response in my ear so I could pass His words on to Carl. I prayed that I wouldn't "wear" this, as I lacked the professional ability to solve his problems. I asked that my prayers for Carl be sufficient and my caring be like Christ, with His love and compassion.

I found I was hesitant every time the phone rang. I'd be thinking, *Is it Carl? What shall I say? What can I do?*

Bernie and I chatted about him and about Jan's death.

"You can only do what you're doing," he said gently. That helped.

That same day at mid-morning, Carl appeared at the door. I didn't recognize him at first. He'd gained so much weight since I'd last seen him and his hair was much longer.

God was good as I relaxed into *true* compassion for Carl. We hugged tightly as I expressed my sorrow at his loss. I told him he was in our prayers and shared that I had once lost a friend to suicide who was the same age as Jan, so I *really* understood how he was feeling.

He asked if I had pictures of he and Jan together, but I hadn't taken any. I did give him the obituary with Jan's photo on it, but not the newspaper article about her jumping in front of the train. He said that he and his caseworker, who was outside waiting for him in her car, were going to get some flowers and go to a park for a little ceremony, as her family wouldn't tell him where she was buried.[15]

Bernie came up from his workshop and hugged Carl, too. Then Carl and I went outside to talk to his caseworker. I let them both know that we were praying for him and would help in practical ways as able.

Carl had to get back to the hospital and wanted to be obedient so they wouldn't "tie him down." I felt better seeing him—God knew what He was doing—and I believed Carl would survive this. It would just take time.

---

[15] In my heart I wanted to find out for him, but knew I didn't know the whole story. I had to respect Jan's family's wishes.

I felt more at peace, knowing that Carl was in good hands. He was attending grief counselling and had an excellent, experienced caseworker. He also expressed that he wanted to continue to attend church when he got out of the hospital.

Exactly a month after Jan died, he dropped into the office to remind us of the date and to say hello. He seemed to be okay and said he had work and a new place to move into at the end of the month. He asked for some food, which we gave him.

I often think of him these many years later and pray that he found direction in his life and that he came to have a personal relationship with Jesus.

Life and ministry go on. I was alone in the office when a young man named Colin came in and asked if he could have coffee and prayer. He was lonely and missing his family and son, who lived in southern Ontario. As our music director played Christmas music in the sanctuary, I invited Colin to take his coffee and sit in the church to hear the music. He went in and sat alone, listening.

A while later, he came back to the office and said that he felt he was being led to share his story with me and asked if I had a few minutes. As busy as I was preparing for our Christmas services, some words I'd sensed God say to me some time ago came quickly to my heart: *"People are not your problem. They are your purpose."*

So I immediately went into the sanctuary with him, praying all the while for the Holy Spirit's leading. I listened to his story and assured him of God's love and forgiveness.

Colin's tears were real as he spoke. Then I felt the strong urge to have him pray, inviting Jesus Christ into his life. He had a rosary in his hands that a lawyer had given him while he was living on the streets.

I led Colin in prayer and he willingly repeated after me: "Father, forgive me for all the wrongs I have done in my life. I now invite Jesus to come into my life and be my Lord and Saviour." With those few, simple words, Colin gave his life to Christ. He sat alone in the church for some time after.

When he came to say goodbye, I suggested that he attend our annual Christmas dinner so he wouldn't be alone. Then I silently prayed, *Thank You, Jesus, for this opportunity to serve, to pray with others and witness for You.*

THE BEST FOR LAST
A Deeper Knowing

IT HAS OFTEN BEEN SAID THAT one saves the best until last and this street friend was one of the best. His story taught me that when you know the Lord, you'll always know what to do if you let God lead. You just have to obediently follow.

This individual also showed me in a deeper way just how temporary life on earth is and how important it is to place more value on kingdom purposes than earthly things. Relaying this story to others shows that some folks have deep-rooted reasons and hidden fears that keep them from staying connected with family and loved ones.

This is a story of a true hero who sadly didn't see himself that way.

Of all the years working at Saint G's, Ray was by far my favourite street friend. He was an Indigenous man with a slight build and he had a friendly, clean-shaven face. His clothes were always neat, he was well-groomed, and he greeted people every morning with a big smile as he sat on the street beside the church. Most folks passing him on their way to work were delighted with his cheeriness.

The first time I met him, I had pulled into the church laneway. Ray had been sitting in his spot nearby and came over to my car when I parked.

"Hi! I'm Ray," he said with an ear-to-ear grin

I shook his hand, told him my name, and added that I was the new parish secretary.

"Yes, I know," Ray replied, adding that word on the street spreads fast. "I'm in such a good mood today. I'm telling everybody they can have next Monday off!"

I laughed because he was referring to an upcoming statutory holiday that most workers would have had off anyway.

After a couple of months of these cheerful daily greetings, he showed up one day drinking and asked if he could talk. He had started attending a detox program. I held his hands and listened as he cried. The smell of alcohol was overwhelming. He also told me he was suffering from AIDS and that Rev. Dave knew about it. Through tears, he admitted that he was afraid for his life and that he'd been unable to see his kids and grandkids. He also said he was afraid he'd give the disease to others if he got too close to them.

I hugged him and then he left. I hoped he was heading to detox.

He had drooled on me as we and hugged, and I didn't feel very Christian as I washed off my sweater and hands. As I did so, I remembered the initial health warnings from the street ministry nurse. I vowed to keep Ray in my prayers.

In spite of his drinking bouts from time to time, Ray was still a joyful presence outside the church and continued his early morning greetings to all who passed.

As I pulled in the church laneway in mid-December, he showed me some Christmas gifts the passersby had given him: a duffle bag full of warm clothes, a blanket, and a card with fifty dollars.

Then a well-dressed young woman called him over.

"Every morning you speak to me and say hello, and I appreciate that," she said.

She gave him a card with twenty dollars inside. He was grinning from ear to ear, as he usually was, and I could tell he felt loved.

I had tears in my eyes yet wondered why I hadn't felt compelled to give him a gift. I *liked* to believe that I had compassion. I wondered if it was because I listened to him, and others, all year, seeing both their good and bad days, when they were drunk, mouthy, and disorderly.

I became upset with myself for judging him. Was this how a "real" Christian should act towards others? I obviously still didn't understand *unconditional* love.

Christmas came and went without me giving Ray a gift. Then on Valentine's Day, Ray gave me a box of chocolates which someone had given him. He let me read the card, and in it the woman had thanked him for his friendliness and cheerful greetings.

"God is using you right on the street, Ray, to spread good cheer to others!" I told him.

Ray had his *own* street ministry to passersby.

One day, he asked if I would write a letter for him to the Department of Indian and Northern Affairs.[16] He told me that he had worked for them at one time and was entitled to a portion of a federal pay equity grant. I gladly did this favour for him and he was excited about potentially receiving a nice sum of money. He asked if he could use the church address, and I readily agreed.

After a couple of months of waiting, his first pay equity cheque arrived at the church. He was so excited that he shook as he opened the envelope. He had received more than three thousand dollars. A letter was enclosed which stated that he would receive another cheque with added interest.

He was thrilled. "I'm going to get a new warm jacket, and then I'm going to go crazy like a white man!"

I roared with laughter and then thanked God for Ray and his loveable personality.

The same day he got his first cheque, he returned to the church before I left for home and brought me a box of long-stemmed yellow roses. They were beautifully packaged from a local florist with a nice handwritten card. I was flabbergasted!

"You did so much for me," he said, "writing letters and making calls for my cheque. I wanted to thank you."

I didn't know what to say. I hugged and thanked him for his kindness.

I thought about leaving the roses in the office but felt that would just draw attention. Everyone would ask about them and I'd have to say why I'd received them and who they were from. So I decided to take them home and tell only my husband.

---

[16] It's now called Indigenous and Northern Affairs Canada.

As I arranged the lovely yellow roses in my dining room vase, I thought, *The roses are so beautiful, but what a waste of Ray's money. They last such a short time.*

Immediately the Holy Spirit brought to mind the story of the woman who poured the expensive perfume over Jesus's head. The disciples argued that her action was such a waste and that the perfume could have been sold and the money given to the poor. But Jesus had told them the woman had done a *"beautiful thing"* (Mark 14:6). My eyes filled with tears as I recognized that Ray had just done a beautiful thing.

Thank You for the lesson, Lord, to just accept gifts of love without questioning.

A couple of days later, Ray came in to show me his new, warm heavy-duty work boots. I was happy to see that he'd spent some money on himself. I gave him a thank-you note for the roses and told him they were still beautiful and thriving.

Ray started attending our midweek early morning communion service. It was so nice to have him there.

One time after the service Ray knelt alone at the altar, crying and upset. I asked if I could kneel beside him and he nodded. He talked about his illness, then told me he hadn't been feeling well and that it was starting to get to him. He shared that his doctor wanted him in hospital, but that he didn't want to go and that he personally felt that he didn't have long to live.

As I listened to his tearful concern, I realized that he hadn't been his usual self lately; the bubbly laughter had been noticeably missing.

Over the years I'd known him, he'd talked little about his family. He'd only told me that he was from a nearby reserve and that he hadn't seen his family in several years. He often told me that he would be going away for a few days and would mention Texas or New York, other places where he supposedly had family.

But it was difficult to know if his stories were true, as some of the details didn't add up from one story to the next.

One time he told me that he was moving to Texas. I asked if I could take his photo to remember him. He agreed and gave his usual big grin as I snapped his picture. That photo was to later prove very significant in someone else's life.

But Ray didn't go after all. I wasn't surprised when one of our parishioners told me she had seen him on the street when he was supposed to be in Texas. I grasped then that he seemed to be hiding and running from something or someone.

Around that time, I also learned that he actually had an apartment but didn't want anyone to know, which is why he lived daily on the streets.

As though nothing had happened, Ray showed up with a Christmas gift for me. He had made me a large dreamcatcher. He also gave me a lovely card with incredible words about Christian love and had signed it "Your friend always, Ray." I was greatly moved to tears once again. I knew I needed to accept God's grace for these expressions of Christian love.

I had grown really worried about Ray as he was losing weight quite rapidly. He shared with me that his stomach, liver, and bowel had all become affected. He gave me his doctor's name, as well as the names of two of his close friends, and asked me to let them know if anything happened to him. I came to accept that Ray didn't have much time left.

Within a few days, I arrived at work to find a note on my desk telling me that Ray was in hospital. I wasn't surprised because he had looked awful the previous week and had been having trouble moving around with a bloated stomach.

I waited for a couple of days to visit, as I had a terrible cold and didn't want to give him my germs. When I finally arrived at the hospital, I discovered that he had been discharged and sent home.

Thankfully, he called me the following day. I was elated to hear from him, but he told me that he was declining fast and now needed a walker to get around. I let him know that several passersby and people from the congregation had been asking for him. I asked if he needed anything. He said that a friend, a fellow I'd met before, was checking on him every day. I was glad to hear that. I mailed him a praying-for-you card with a scripture booklet inside.

His friend called a few days later to say that Ray wanted to talk. But as hard as I tried, I really couldn't understand him as he was very incoherent. He sounded heavily drugged and very weak.

I let Rev. Dave know and he decided he'd better go see him right away. I asked if I could go along with him, since I really wanted to see Ray, too, but didn't want to go alone. After calling Ray's friend at his apartment, we made arrangements to visit that afternoon.

Arriving in the building, Rev. Dave and I prayed together in the hallway before knocking on his door. His friend let us in and there was Ray sitting in a chair with a blanket wrapped around his shoulders. We were shocked at his appearance. He was gaunt and skeletal. His hair was much longer and he had stubble for a beard. His abdomen was swollen and distended and his eyes large and bulging.

Initially he recognized us and seemed alert, but during our visit his attention would drift and he'd become incoherent and rambling. At one alert point, Ray was able to receive communion from Rev. Dave. It was a very special sharing time and I was so glad we had visited.

Both Rev. Dave and I were grateful that Ray's friend was staying with him. A nurse also visited every day.

I hugged him goodbye, knowing that I wouldn't see him alive again. Ray would be missed.

My husband was interested in hearing about our visit with Ray, as the whole story had touched Bill's heart. When I'd told him the previous week that Ray was dying from AIDS, my husband said genuinely, "I'd help him if I could." That was nice to hear. I knew God had done some work in changing Bill's heart toward street people, as well as those suffering from AIDS.

My prayers for Ray changed from healing to asking God to take him to Himself so his suffering would be over. Two days after our visit with him, his friend called to say that Ray had been sent to hospital the previous day and had passed away through the night.

Ray's friend told me that he was having a difficult time locating relatives. However, after searching through some paperwork, he had found Ray's birth certificate which indicated his place of birth on the reserve he had often talked about. I suggested the friend call the reserve chief and I offered to help as I could.

I called Rev. Dave to let him know about Ray's passing. We were both saddened but so glad that we had gone to visit with him when we did!

Ray was sixty-four when he died and I knew he would be missed by a lot of people. I suddenly remembered the picture I had taken of Ray a couple of years previously and retrieved it. He looked so healthy with his big smile. I asked Bernie to make a large sign to put in the church laneway so we could let the people whom Ray had greeted daily know of his passing. We also made up a framed poster to put on the church bulletin board to inform our parishioners; they had grown to love Ray over the years.

The following Sunday in church, I had a sense of loneliness over Ray's death. The reading was about the crippled beggar who had sat outside the temple for years. Peter didn't give him money but instead made him whole, and he walked again because of God's love (Acts 3).

It was a timely reading. The story reminded me of Ray, as he had sat outside Saint G's for many years. We hadn't given him money, but we had given him love—and he us.

A couple of days after Ray's death, I received a call from a funeral director. He told me they had located Ray's sister, Sharon, on the reserve. Thank You, God, for answered prayer! The family quickly arranged to have a visitation and funeral in Ottawa for family and friends.

When I arrived at the funeral home, Ray's close friend was out front with another mutual friend who was greatly distressed, as he'd just found out the previous day about Ray's death. They were talking to a young Indigenous fellow (in full buckskin attire), a young woman, and an older woman who I just knew had to be Ray's sister. The resemblance was undeniable!

I was introduced to Sharon. She was the spitting image of Ray, albeit shorter and a little pudgier. She shyly puffed on her cigarette, shook my hand, and introduced me to her son, the young man wearing the buckskins.

"This was Ray's only nephew and his godson," she said by way of introduction. "We've been looking for Ray for over twelve years. We've looked everywhere, including the internet."

I was happy to learn that Ray had been loved and searched for, yet at the same time very sad that he had felt the need to hide from his family, missing out on twelve years of family closeness and their love.

Sharon gave me a brief verbal biography of Ray's life. He was the baby of the family, and he had a wife and son and now two grandchildren. Ray had previously told us a somewhat different story about his past.

Sharon continued, letting me know that Ray had been a sergeant in the U.S. Marines and had served in Vietnam. She had all his military paperwork and medals at her home, along with other personal papers. He had moved back to the reserve for a time after Vietnam and then the chief had brought him to Ottawa to get him work at Indian and Northern Affairs. This was the only part of Ray's story that I actually knew about, as this was the federal department that had sent his pay equity cheques.

I had put the photo I had taken of Ray into a small frame and brought it along with me. I wanted to offer it to Sharon, but I waited for the right time—and it came when she said that Ray looked so thin that she hardly recognized him. I pulled the framed photo from my purse and said, "I took this a couple of years ago. You may have it if you'd like." She gladly took it and said, "Oh yes, I would. This is how I remember him!"

God is so good. He takes care of even the smallest details. Only God would have known why the photo had been meant to be taken two years ago.

I excused myself and went inside to see Ray. There were about eight other people in the visitation room, all from the reserve. As I went over to the coffin, his nephew joined me. Ray really did look good; the funeral directors had packed his hollow cheeks so his face looked fuller. He was dressed in a lovely black suit with white shirt and tie and looked so sophisticated. A rather small buckskin vase rested across his chest with some feathers in it and a red cloth above his hands.

I asked his nephew the significance of these items.

"The red cloth was wrapped around special tobacco," he said. "When Ray gets cremated, it will burn as well; then the feather can be used to symbolically fan away all the bad spirits so Ray goes directly to God."

I found that very touching.

"If the viewing had been on the reserve, then everyone who came to visit would add a feather to the holder," the nephew further explained.

That seemed like such a nice personal gesture.

The reserve chief came over and introduced himself. He was very polite, friendly, and articulate. He had a commanding presence and was well-dressed in a black suit, with jet-black hair. He introduced me to his own brother.

As I talked to them, I spoke of how Ray had been an "ambassador" on the street outside our church, how friendly he had been and how everyone had loved him. I mentioned that Ray had often attended our Wednesday morning Eucharist and had often come into the church, knelt at the altar, and prayed—sometimes alone, and if he was in distress we'd pray together.

Immediately the Chief said, "You have to tell Sharon this!" He led me over to Ray's sister once again and I repeated what I had just said. This information offered Sharon great comfort. I realized at this point that many of these people were Christians.

Sharon shared that Ray had been an altar boy and had sung in the choir. Then Ray's uncle gave me a postcard of the little stone church on their reserve. They were obviously very proud of the church, as it had been designated Chapel Royale by Queen Elizabeth when she had visited in 2002.

From that point on, our conversation was about the church. It was so nice to know that Ray had known the Lord for quite a while and that his sister was very comforted to know that he had a church connection. I enjoyed our conversation and the opportunity to meet these wonderful people.

There were only about twenty of us at the cathedral for Ray's funeral and our chatter echoed in the large sanctuary. It was a lovely service from the Anglican Book of Common Prayer. We sang two hymns, one of them being "How Great Thou Art." During communion, the chief, his brother, and Ray's uncle sang Psalm 23 in their own tongue; it was incredibly powerful as the words rose and echoed around us. It took me back to when Ray had prayed in his own language during our prayer times together.

The chief read a poem Ray had sent to his mother while he was stationed in Vietnam. It talked about serving God and country and how horrible it really had been over there. The poem ended with "And when I reach the pearly gates, Saint Peter will say, 'Come in, my son—you've already been through hell.'"

That line said it all for me. Now I understood Ray's torment and why I had seen him recoil one time when cornered by a policeman who was really only trying to help him.

Outside the church, we said our goodbyes. The chief thanked me for all I had done and Sharon gave me a huge hug. We had closure and Ray was going home, his ashes to be buried on his beloved reserve.

"Goodbye, old friend," I whispered as I got into my car. "It was a pleasure knowing you. I trust you are with Jesus, so I know I'll see you again someday."

ALL WORTHWHILE
One Came Back

WHAT A SURPRISE... STANLEY SHOWED UP again! It had been three years since we'd last seen him, and he looked fantastic. He wasn't the same dishevelled man we had previously known. He'd put on weight, had clean hair, and was neatly dressed in new casual clothes.

"I just came in to say hello," he said with a broad smile. He shared that he'd been living in the same city where he'd been living the last time I heard from him. He spoke sensibly and said he was grateful for all the peanut butter sandwiches we had given him. "They kept me going."

His visit made my day, as I'd been wondering if he was dead or alive. In my heart, I was so thankful that he had been one of the survivors.

There were so many things we as a church, and other inner-city ministries, tried to do over the years to minister to street friends. There were, and continue to be, so many occasions when we probably won't ever know the end result of our spending time with street folks, whether it's giving them a glass of cold water, making a sandwich, offering warm clothes, listening, laughing, crying, and/or praying with them.

But like the lepers in Scripture, out of the ten that were healed only one came back to give praise to God (Luke 17:11–19). We never offered this ministry to be thanked, but instead to be His hands and feet and to point people to God, to whom the praise truly belongs. And like the one leper who did come back, I knew that if only one street friend recognized that God had worked in them, it made all the years of service to the fragile in our community well worthwhile.

Many times over the years of working at Saint G's, I had to ask the Lord to forgive me for judging some of the walk-in clientele. I needed help to see them through Jesus's eyes and treat them with His love and compassion.

I regretted that before working at the church I'd looked upon some folks as coming from the bottom of the sea, bottom-feeders and leeches, but God saw them as fish of many kinds. He gave me the opportunity to gather them in His net at Saint G's, to minister to their practical and spiritual needs and learn to do so *without* judging.

As Christians, we are called to be God's fishermen and catch "fish" for Him. In our interactions with people, our "nets" may become full of many different kinds that we may not think are worthy of keeping, but it is not up to us to judge, as everyone is important to the Lord and in need of saving.

In Scripture, it is written:

For I was hungry and you gave me food, I was thirsty and you gave me drink, I was a stranger and you welcomed me, I was naked and you clothed me, I was sick and you visited me, I was in prison and you came to me. (Matthew 25:35–36)

Both my husband and I learned that street people aren't bums who need a job. Rather, they are God's people, with names and faces. People in desperate need. Thank You, Jesus, for the opportunity to have lived out these words in service to the street folks *You* love. I know I'll continue to look for others to help throughout the years I have left on this side of heaven.

Mother Teresa once said,

"Stay where you are. Find your own Calcutta. Find the sick, the suffering, and the lonely, right where you are—in your own homes and in your own families, in homes and in your workplaces and in your schools. You can find Calcutta all over the world, if you have eyes to see. Everywhere, wherever you go, you find people who are unwanted, unloved, uncared for, just rejected by society—completely forgotten, completely left alone."[17]

Jesus needs to know that He has servants on the earth who are available and willing to act when He calls them to do something. He needs faithful soldiers to be His hands, feet, and voice here. Our role is to make ourselves available, to wait, listen, hear, and obey as He leads.

May God open your heart and lead you into service to all those for whom Christ died. The Holy Spirit will empower and strengthen you for the tasks. To God be the glory!

---

[17] Erika Glover, "Live Like Mother Teresa: Finding Your Own Calcutta," *Franciscan Spirit*. March 13, 2018 (https://www.franciscanmedia.org/franciscan-spirit-blog/live-like-mother-teresa-finding-your-own-calcutta). Quoting Mother Teresa.

ABOUT THE AUTHOR

MARCIA MAGEE MCCLELLAND IS A DEVOUT Christian and a former parish administrator at St. George's Anglican Church (now St. Peter and St. Paul's) in Ottawa, Ontario. Born and raised in Saint John, New Brunswick, she has lived in Ontario since 1973 and is the proud mother of two adult daughters. She delights in being "G-ma" to four young adult grandchildren. She and her husband Bill live in a small village on the outskirts of Ottawa where she enjoys volunteering where needed, gardening in the summer, artwork in the winter, and writing in her journal year-round! This is her second published book. She is also the author of *The Great Gift Idea Book*, published in 1987 by Gai-Garet Design and Publication.

She can be reached through email at mbmcclel@magma.ca.

www.ingramcontent.com/pod-product-compliance
Lightning Source LLC
LaVergne TN
LVHW051421080426
835508LV00022B/3191